FAR FLUNG
Floyd

FAR FLUNG
Floyd

KEITH FLOYD'S GUIDE
TO SOUTH-EAST ASIAN FOOD

A Citadel Press Book
Published by Carol Publishing Group

I would like to dedicate this book to:

the management and staff of the Imperial Family Group of
Hotels in Thailand

the people of Vietnam

Hafiz and Awi and the people of Malaysia

Shaunagh Floyd – isn't there a saying: 'Behind every great
... (?!) there is a greater woman'

I would also like to acknowledge the help of Fiona Harris

First Carol Publishing Group Edition - 1994

Published by arrangement with Michael Joseph Ltd, London, England.

A Citadel Press Book
Published by Carol Publishing Group
Citadel Press is a registered trademark of Carol Communications, Inc.
Editorial Offices: 600 Madison Avenue, New York, NY 10022
Sales & Distribution Offices: 120 Enterprise Avenue, Secaucus, NJ 07094
In Canada: Canadian Manda Group, P.O. Box 920, Station U, Toronto,
Ontario, M8Z 5P9, Canada
Queries regarding rights and permissions should be addressed to:
Carol Publishing Group, 600 Madison Avenue, New York, NY 10022

Recipe Photographer: James Murphy
Home Economist: Berit Vinegrad
Stylist: Roisin Nield
Cookery Adviser: Valerie Barrett
Illustrator: Jane Brewster

Manufactured in the United States of America
ISBN 0-8065-1523-6

10 9 8 7 6 5 4 3 2 1

Carol Publishing Group books are available at special discounts
for bulk purchases, for sales promotions, fund raising, or
educational purposes. Special editions can also be created to
specifications. For details contact: Special Sales Department,
Carol Publishing Group, 120 Enterprise Ave., Secaucus, NJ 07094

Library of Congress Cataloging-in-Publication Data

Floyd, Keith.
     Far flung Floyd : Keith Floyd's guide to South-East Asian food.
     p.   cm.
     "A Citadel Press book."
      1. Cookery, Southeast Asian.   I. Title.
TX724.5.S68F58   1994
641.5959–dc20   93-45392
                                 CIP

CONTENTS

MALAYSIA

EASTWARD BOUND

With a fair wind, the journey from Floyd's Inn, Tuckenhay, in deepest darkest Devon, to the bar of the Sebel Town House Hotel in Sydney, Australia, takes about thirty-four hours – glass to glass. However many times you have made the journey, and I have done it a great deal, it is extremely tiring, and despite your high spirits and excitement at seeing old friends again, the following day jet lag hits you hard. It is as if someone has thrown you from the parapet of a high building into a mattress of cotton wool. Which, though it does not hurt you, envelops and suffocates you and leaves you struggling vainly against dreams in a disturbing half-sleep.

So this little jaunt to Malaysia, via Bangkok and Singapore courtesy of Qantas, first leg of the Far Flung Floyd tour, should have been a doddle in comparison. The journey to Heathrow was swift and uneventful. Rob Page (our executive producer) was at the airport, gave us presents, wished us luck and waved us goodbye. And with a happy heart my wife Shaunagh and I toddled to the first-class cabin (naturally) of the Boeing 747, destination Bangkok.

I was greeted at the entrance door by the (ahem, ahem, clear throat, cough) in-flight service director, who said, 'G'day, Floydie, welcome back.' Now to many international first-class travellers this attitude does not go down too well, but I thoroughly enjoy flying Qantas because it is so relaxed and cheerful, although I think on this particular flight they were a little miffed because British Airways seemed to have bought about twenty-five per cent of their company.

However, we were soon into the champagne and a dish of assorted nuts – macadamia, cashews, peanuts, Brazils – which I absolutely detest. This is a Travel-cum-Cookbook for general readership so I won't be able to recount the joke that the head stewardess (note, stewardess) told me about oral sex as she garnished my fillet of salmon with a sprig of parsley!

Anyway, after a couple of movies, a couple of meals, it was Shaunagh's turn this time to go on the flight deck to land the plane in Bangkok. A couple of drinks with the kitchen staff and a stroll down to the back end of the plane to see the poor people – by that I mean my director and cameraman etc., etc., – and there we were, as it were, in a trice in Bangkok, waiting for the next plane to take us to Singapore. We did no duty-free shopping for with two months ahead of us we'd have all the time we needed to buy silks and have suits made.

The whole gang of us – that is to say: David Pritchard (director); Kora McNulty (our production assistant, who doubled as David's nanny, and may I say she did a brilliant job); Paul Otter (camera); Steve Williams (lighting and sanity); Tim White (sound and worldwide authority); Shaunagh (food co-ordinator and my nanny); and Me – trundled up to the first-class lounge and cheerfully gave the complimentary bar a good hiding. This happy band, some would say this motley crew, only come together once a year. And we always set off full of enthusiasm, with high hopes and – for the moment at least – an unshakable sense of camaraderie.

We toasted absent friends, to wit, the great Clive North, cameraman on all of the previous Floyd programmes except one, and Andy McCormack, previous assistant cameraman and ambassador to the Court of New Age Travellers. None of us was in any way prepared to admit why these two had refused to come on this particular trip. They always said they had enjoyed themselves before. But the truth of it was they have both progressed so far in their careers that we were unable to match the kind of money they were now making. Privately I was worried about not having Clive as I had worked so closely with him over the years. It was going to be very strange working with another cameraman who may have different ideas and a different attitude. But David was much more philosophical and optimistic about it. 'It will give the programmes,' he said, 'a much-needed injection of fresh ideas.'

Finally, the flight was called and off we tramped down endless passageways in Bangkok airport, to board the plane for Singapore. And a quick flight, only a couple of hours, saw us all once again in the first-class lounge at Singapore airport. People were still cheerful, of course, but were now having teas, coffees and soft drinks. Conversation was less garrulous; in fact, it was muted. Four hours dragged by slowly at Singapore airport. David, affectionately known to the in-flight staff at Qantas airlines as Mr Chardonnay, was having what doubtless he considered to be a very well-earned snooze. The flight was called, David was asked to wake up and his first words, later to become so familiar we hardly noticed them, were: 'Kora, where is my suitcase, where is my passport?'

We settled resignedly into our seats, declined the pre-take-off champagne and later declined dinner – or was it lunch or was it tea or was it breakfast? I tried really hard to watch the film but sleep overcame me and I awoke to hear a soft, sweet voice saying, first in English and then in a variety of other tongues, 'Ladies and gentlemen, we are about to make our final descent into Kuala Lumpur international airport. Local time is ... The temperature is ... And ladies and gentlemen, I would like to remind you that in Malaysia the penalty for trafficking in drugs is death. Thank you for flying with Malaysian Airlines, we trust you have enjoyed your flight and that we can be of service to you soon. Good evening.'

Until this point our personal luggage and one hundred and twenty-two pieces of equipment had been shipped direct. For the first time we now had to go through customs and transfer to the domestic airport for our ultimate flight of the day. There was nothing very much international about Kuala Lumpur's international airport. It was hot and humid and I – something of a Jeremiah from time to time on these trips – had resigned myself to the worst. Like my old friend Hector used to say, 'Hope for the best but fear the worst'.

However, a director of the Malaysian Tourist Board, a bubbly, thirty-year-old, frightfully well-spoken gentleman called Hafiz, was there to greet us and we passed through customs swiftly. What seemed like hundreds of porters were summoned and mountains of aluminium boxes were piled high and with grunts and shouts were shifted round to the domestic terminal. This was crowded with army officers in uniform, businessmen with gold chains round their wrists and medallions round their necks, people with fezzes, Muslim women in full dress – brilliantly coloured silk robes neck-to-toe with their white headgear, called *telekung*, Australians in their shorts and T-shirts, neat Americans, spotty, long-haired hippies and, so help me God, a few British businessmen in their Burton director suits, clutching imitation Burberry raincoats and looking hot, uncomfortable and ill at ease. Dutch, Germans and Japanese – all fresh and chattering, in neatly pressed lightweight suits – clutched briefcases and talked dollars. The first-class lounge was packed with this noisy, oddly smelling mass of international travellers. Aftershaves, anti-perspirant deodorants, henna – every conceivable perfume intermingled with sweat.

There was a buffet in the corner and a couple of women frying rice and noodles. On the small rotisserie, little curried tartlets spun slowly round. This, I thought, is a real airport, this one isn't just for leaving and arriving, it is one used for going places and doing things.

After an hour we found ourselves checking our watches, looking at the departure board and straining our ears for the near-incomprehensible announcements of departures and arrivals. Plane after plane departed and there was no mention of ours. A half-hour and another half-hour. We were beginning to worry, had we missed the announcement? Finally, there was only us and half-a-dozen others left, and the whole place, which an hour ago had been mayhem, now looked like one of the temporary bars at Cheltenham after the last race on Gold Cup Day.

It was time to board and David was missing. Kora volunteered to find him. He was apparently on his way back to the international terminal, looking for his bag and presumably his passport – both of which Kora already had. At last, this now quite weary band shambled through the blistering heat, made worse by a hot, hot wind, on to the Malaysian Airlines DC 10 or whatever it was. Which, after the wide-bodied jumbos, seemed like a tinny, tiny bone-shaker, like something you used to pay five shillings at a fair to sit in and go round in circles.

It was a domestic flight, it was a No Smoking flight, it was Malaysian, it was a dry flight. For supper or breakfast or lunch or tea or dinner, they gave us a puff pastry pie that when cut open revealed three things – a thick smear of curry paste, an expanse of uncooked pastry, and a couple of peas and a few cubes of carrot. And a glass of, Lord help me, most inappropriate for my mood at least, a glass of passion-fruit juice.

We flew for at least two hours through the night and, peering out of the window, I could see nothing but black. No lights, no towns, no motorways, nothing. I nodded off fitfully and woke up – as you all know, when you fly a lot you instinctively know when you are going round and round and round in circles. I checked my watch and realised we should have landed twenty minutes earlier. Finally, the plane straightened out and began to descend. All of a sudden we could see the faint lights of the large urban sprawl of Terengganu, north-east Malaysia – with the under-powered lighting that I was to become very used to over the next few months.

We assembled in the baggage claim area and Glenys, our production manager, was there to meet us. But not the promised vehicles, to wit a truck for the crew's equipment, the minibus for the crew and a car for me. There was pandemonium. The crew, used to being buggered about and probably the most patient travellers in the world, were showing signs, unusual for them, of real frustration and annoyance. Where were the vehicles, why weren't they here? Glenys was darting around, our interpreter could speak Malay but not English and confusion reigned. And I, I have to say, was getting very irate.

Then Kora took charge of Shaunagh and me and bundled us into a taxi, assuring us that the taxi driver had been paid. But, in my Jeremiah way, I demanded money just in case. And we drove off into the night in a bouncy, battered taxi with ripped upholstery, door handles missing and windows obscured by No Smoking signs. Thus began a harrowing two-hour journey on ill-lit, ill-marked, badly-surfaced roads, with a driver who chose to overtake unlit water-buffalo-drawn carts on corners, and unlit motorcycles, with three or four people on them, on the inside. He spoke no English, we no Malay. There was no means of communication, we didn't know where we were going, and little by little we fell silent and not a little afraid.

Half an hour passed, surely the hotel must be soon, I thought. Another half-hour, another fifteen minutes. We must surely be there. On and on and on we went, passing here and there a roadside hamlet with dimly lit shacks all emitting a curious, unearthly green glow. Shadowy figures moved behind rattan blinds. Then we turned off this, what must have been, for all that, main road and I thought perhaps this is where he is going to dump us, steal our luggage and drive off. And I prepared myself for some kind of self-defence.

However, round another corner, lit in a blaze of white light, we entered a tree-lined, smooth Tarmac driveway. Each tree was festooned with literally hundreds and hundreds of small white light bulbs. It was so breathtakingly pretty that I almost exclaimed 'How beautiful'. But instead I said to myself, 'It had better be a decent hotel after all this fucking way'. We drove to reception. My heart sank. The place was a perfect replica of a Malay chief's palace – open walled, massive teak verandahs and open roofs, but I knew at once it was not a hotel. It was a resort. When you are working you need hotels that have twenty-four-hour room service, faxes, telephones, business centres. However awful the food is, it doesn't matter as long as you have these facilities.

We were welcomed with great enthusiasm and told to load our baggage on to a trolley. They insisted we see our room straightaway. It was five to eleven at night. We had been travelling for thirty-six hours, longer than it takes to get to the Sebel Town House in Sydney. We had travelled half the distance and all we wanted was a bloody large drink.

A TRIP TO DUNGUN MARKET

I spent a restless night in our gloomy wooden Malay longhouse due to a combination of jet lag, a hastily eaten, indifferent curry for supper at midnight, and the discordant jangling of the duo – a boy and girl team, he on synthesised keyboards, she on vocals, and their cover versions of 'Never On A Sunday' and 'Fly Me To The Moon' – which repeated through my brain all night long and resulted in my waking up feeling sick and tired. Plus the ancient air-conditioning, pitter-pattering all night long like the winter rain on the slate roof of my home in Devon made for, all in all, a rotten night.

In the half light of early morning I fumbled with a variety of doors – heavy, beautiful teak doors with brass furniture (door furniture that is) of a nautical style – and eventually found a huge bathroom. Actually, it wasn't a bathroom because there was no bath. There was a massive shower rose and a couple of mildewy big brass taps, and in the corner there was a stone trough with hot and cold taps over it, a plastic bucket hanging from one of them. The idea being that you filled up the trough and chucked buckets of water over you for a quick sluice. Great in theory, but not practical in reality, because there was no hot water. So I gave myself a cat-lick with cold water and dressed in my 'Sanders of the River' outfit – to wit, lace-up leather boots, beige socks, Desert Rat-style shorts and a near-khaki shirt with a vague military cut. And with Shaunagh attired in a well-cut light blue linen safari suit, we stepped into the daylight, headed for breakfast.

In a trice tiredness and gloom evaporated. Only yards from our cabin, or hut or whatever you like to call it, long slow breakers of the

South China Sea crashed on to a beautiful white sand beach. Monkeys jumped between the palms and vividly coloured birds swooped and screeched between the trees. There were probably thirty or forty cabins dotted around the main complex, all of them constructed in traditional Malay-style, that is to say, built on stilts and with long verandahs facing the sea. Lying awake one moment during the night, I had noticed a little white tag nailed high in the vaulted roof of our room, indicating east, so that the good Muslim on holiday knew which way to kneel at prayers.

We took breakfast on an enormous verandah that overlooked a landscaped garden of luxuriant trees, shrubs and pretty man-made ponds. Breakfast was a choice from the Malaysian buffet – fried rice, curried meat, noodles, tropical fruits. But for the first and what was to be the last time, we opted for a European-style breakfast.

The sky was now heavy with cloud and it was impossibly warm. Any day now – it was the middle of November – the rainy season would start, and so the hotel/resort had very few guests. The tourist authorities of Malaysia have forbidden the more traditional word, 'monsoon', because it was found to be bad for business. Presently we were introduced to Awi, who was to be my driver and guide for the whole of the Malaysian leg. He was a charming, open and friendly man of about thirty-eight, with a neatly pressed short-sleeved white shirt, black trousers and immaculately shiny shoes. He walked with the rolling gait of a seaman. We got on famously from the first. His helpfulness, his tolerance of constantly changing schedules and locations, and his knowledge of all things Malaysian – both gastronomically and culturally – were extraordinary.

We decided to visit the nearby town of Dungun to try to get a bit of a feel for the place. We had thoughtfully been provided with a stretched version of Malaysia's home-produced car, the Proton. In shape it represented the Cadillacs you see at airports in American films. But, curiously enough, there was only room for two in the back, the rest of the seats being taken up by a television, refrigerators and telephones. But it was fun. It was a sort of pocket limousine.

We set off along the palm-fringed coast road with occasional glimpses of the ocean and small fishermen's *kampongs* (villages). There were little groups of simple hardwood houses set on stilts where chickens and ducks scratched happily away underneath. Here and there along the road would be an enormous iron pot steaming over a wood fire. Old ladies squatting beside a neatly stacked pyramid of sweetcorn were cooking them, to sell to the passing traveller. Now and again there was a three-sided shack with rolled-up rattan blinds piled high with dried fish, plastic tableware and bowls, cheap tin cooking utensils, crates of root beer and other comestibles.

There was not much traffic but progress was slow because of the unmarked and untethered Walt Disney cows of the area, which wandered aimlessly up and down or across the road. And there were cats everywhere, really charming small furry purrynesses that had no tails, just short stumps. Wickedly, I wondered for an idle moment whether this was the result of a Malay prediliction for cats' tails, but I was assured that they were as nature had intended!

Dungun was a quaint little town with mainly single-storey buildings. Towards the centre, where there were slightly bigger warehouses and administration blocks, it had a faint air of having once been a British garrison town. This part of Malaysia is strictly Muslim and the women were dressed accordingly, but in splendid colours – vermilions, oranges, purples, jade greens and so on. Open-fronted shop houses, apparently mainly run by Chinese, were emporiums of great fascination for me. Here a shop specialising in tin buckets, watering cans and cooking pots, with a couple of old men sitting cross-legged on the floor cutting sheets of tin and beating them into these exquisite simple utensils. There another shop with five or six women peddling furiously at Singer sewing machines, running up various garments. Another filled with high-standing fans in pale 1950s' colours – pale pinks, greens, blues, mauves – with their shiny chromium-plated faces turning like sunflowers to the sun.

Noodle shops with cauldrons of stock and mountains of noodles on stainless steel tables. And the whoosh of pressurised paraffin that fired the massive rings underneath the pots. And still the cattle and the cats and sheep wandered through the town, oblivious of all around them.

There was a store selling water pumps and hosepipes. Jubilee clips. Another stacked floor to ceiling with woks. And shops filled with coconut graters.

Another store was stacked floor to ceiling with wooden pallets containing what looked like galvanised iron buckets, each lined with murky brown terracotta. On the top, inside, was a simple, circular, removable baked clay grill. And on the side, there was a small air vent for controlling the heat. These unprepossessing charcoal burners are the most versatile cookers I have encountered. They generate enough heat to stir-fry with a wok, and they burn long and slow enough to make a perfect Beef Rendang. Here they cost less than £3 each. They don't blow out in the wind, and they are widely used throughout south-east Asia.

In fact, these stoves were so good that I later abandoned our mighty BBC wok machine in favour of one of these. But for the sake of truth and honesty, I must say it was not until David manoeuvred me into using one on a wooden fishing rig in the Straits of Malacca that I was convinced they were as good as everyone said. Now when we go to Ascot, Henley and Cheltenham and various other sportin' events, I insist that our cook prepares our picnic on one. I have even gone to great lengths so that it won't damage the boot of the Bentley, by commissioning a hand-made leather travelling box for it! At one stage, I was so enthused by the charcoal burners that I thought I would ship several back to my pub in Devon. But wiser counsel prevailed. Bearing in mind that we have no one in the pub capable even of lighting an open fire in the bar, there would be absolutely no chance of anybody being able to keep one of these little beauties going. Only a joke, Mel!

We wandered through the market, spectacular and smelly, hot and crowded. The tang of salted fish, the stomach-turning aroma of fish intestines, and the sweet dusty perfume of stack after stack after stack of rice – long-grain, short-grain, husked and non-husked. Just to stand there, amid this intensity, this throng of people buying a few grams of ginger, a kilo of fishheads, a sprig of chicken's feet or two or three lime leaves, was amazing. And everybody saying, 'Hello, are you from England?' There was a curious walled-off area of the market. Here, behind high walls and out of sight of the faithful Muslims, was the pork butchery department for the non-Muslims, that is, the Chinese community.

My main purpose for being here was to shop for my first cooking sketch. In a hardware shop I bought gas fittings for my portable wok machine. And, led by some strange power, I entered a Chinese emporium that had glass windows and a glass door where I found, to my childish delight, in between shelves of beancurd, soy sauce and curious spices, jars of Heinz sandwich spread, tins of Jacobs' cream crackers, tinned English butter and Cadburys' chocolate. So for a hilarious fifteen minutes I shopped nostalgically 'till I could carry no more.

Some Notes on Malaysian Cooking

However, back to the market and to Malay cooking. This has been strongly influenced by the Chinese and the Indians and, of course, the Arabs, who left a heavy Islamic imprint on the food.

■ There is also Nonya cuisine, created by the intermarriage of Malay women and Chinese men. This is more evident in the south than it is in the east. It is Chinese-style food, but pepped up with the Malaysian fondness for fiery spices.

■ Where we were, in the north-east, pig is not eaten for religious reasons. The main source of meat is chicken and buffalo. Curries of one kind or another are very much the business with the local Malay people. Less so with the Chinese.

■ And Awi told me that one of the most popular dishes around is Chicken with Tamarind – a spice which, I must admit, I had never encountered before, bar in Worcestershire Sauce. Well, tamarind on the hoof, so to speak, looks a bit like a knobbly broad bean. It grows to about four inches in length and is harvested when the brittle shell is a light brown colour and is beginning to crack. Inside are little black seeds surrounded by a sour, fruity pulp.

Commercially you can obtain it quite easily, certainly in Asian food-stores in Britain. It is often sold packed, stones and all, in small plastic blocks, which look a bit like squidgy dates. If you obtain it this way, you must take the required amount and soak it in hot water before adding it to your chosen dish. With your fingers you then separate the stones from the pulp and strain off the liquid so you have tamarind water. But the best way to buy it is as tamarind concentrate, either in a tub or a jar or a small plastic bag. It will look like molasses or that treacly malt children of my generation were made to eat a spoonful of each morning.

■ This useful spice adds flavour and a hint of sourness to a dish, but the Malays like to temper this with a certain amount of sweetness and for this, if you want gastronomic authenticity, you should try and obtain palm sugar. In Malaysia and throughout south-east Asia, you will find discs of palm sugar about four inches in diameter by one inch thick, sugar wrapped in a piece of dried leaf. This makes it look like fudge and, in fact, it has the texture of brittle fudge. I have seen it in plenty of shops in the UK, but if you are unable to find it, then a strong demerara sugar would be an acceptable substitute.

■ Another souring ingredient favoured by the Malaysians is a fish paste, sold in blocks or cakes, which is known as *blacan* and used instead of *nuoc mam*, the liquid version favoured by the Vietnamese and to some extent the Thais. Incidentally, if you are using it, it is very strong and powerful and you should lightly toast it before crumbling it in, like an Oxo cube, to any dish.

■ On the subject of toasting spices, whenever you are cooking with dried seeds – take coriander, for example, as we will in the dish I am about to describe – you can extract so much more flavour from them if you toast them lightly in a dry pan over a low heat for a few moments before you grind them up. Anyway, that is the end of Lesson One.

If you will excuse me for a few moments, I am nipping back into the eating area of the market because earlier I caught a glimpse of an Indian man rolling out small balls of dough, flattening them in discs and then spinning them, pizza-style, into thin circular shapes about twelve inches in diameter. He popped them on to an oiled sheet of steel which sat on top of one of those bucket charcoal stoves. He fried them quickly on both sides, rolled them up, put a spoonful of curry sauce with some chopped hard-boiled egg over the top and sold each for about 2 pence on a scarred plastic plate. That, with a cup of sweet green Malay tea, makes a splendid breakfast.

I seemed to have lost Awi and I couldn't remember where the car was. I reached for the endless flimsy polythene bags full of the produce we had bought, only to find them snatched out of my hand by Awi – who materialised, rather like Jeeves, from absolutely nowhere.

A Cooking Sketch

By the time we returned to the compound – whoops, sorry, I mean the resort, David and Paul had established an ocean-side location in the shade of some tall, swaying coconut palms. I deliberately approached them quietly through the trees without revealing my presence, to make sure that they had already assembled this amazing wok. It weighed about eight tons, came in a custom-built aluminium box about fifty-eight feet wide by forty-nine feet deep and required the muscle of two or three elephants and the combined intelligence of master Mensa members to assemble it. But, of course, this was where Tim always came in; he is so eminently practical. In the middle of the desert, when you suddenly need, of all things, a jubilee clip, incredibly Tim will have one in his little box of tricks.

Now you have to make some concessions to trickery and compromise when you are filming a food programme. And although I genuinely had been shopping for the ingredients I intended to use in the next dish, much earlier in the day Razak, the head chef at the Tanjong Jara Hotel, had jointed a chicken for me and marinated it in a mixture of tamarind water, soy sauce, palm sugar, half-a-dozen cloves of finely chopped garlic and half-a-dozen small shallots, chopped similarly. Because, as I am sure you fully understand, if you started with me behind the wok saying, 'Right, let's make this tamarind juice by pouring boiling water over the stones and squeezing out the juice [which indeed I do say on camera] and now we will pour it over the chicken and leave it for four hours,' we could all become bored sitting there for four hours watching the chicken marinating – so we have to take little short cuts like that from time to time.

But then I do actually cook the recipe for real and we reach a point where I say 'the lid goes on and that simmers away for thirty or forty minutes' and we sit there, pacing up and down the beach or wherever we are, until it is ready. And the reason it has to be authentic at that point is because we invariably invite a passer-by – chauffeur, a fisherman or anybody we can get our hands on – to taste the completed dish. So it has to be up to scratch.

So to proceed with this cooking sketch as if for television. I have my table with all the raw ingredients carefully laid out so that the viewer (my Mum) can see all of the component parts. I joint the chicken and place the pieces in a bowl, then I prepare the tamarind juice properly and correctly and, with the other ingredients I have already mentioned, add to the chicken to marinate.

Then we shift the camera position a little bit to show me toasting two tablespoons or so of coriander seeds. Once they are toasted, I begin to grind them up in a pestle and mortar – in the meantime already having some fully ground in a dish on the floor, out of shot. By the magic of television I substitute my dish of marinated chicken for the one which has already been genuinely marinated, add the coriander, pop the lot into a heavy saucepan and simmer for about forty minutes, or until the chicken pieces are tender and the liquid has reduced, to create a fairly dry curry.

If you make this at home I suggest you serve it with fragrant long-grain rice that you have rinsed three or four times and carefully drained. And instead of using water to boil it in, take a fresh green coconut or two, slice off the tops and pour the clear liquid to one inch above the level of the rice, season with salt, put on a lid and cook gently until there is no liquid left and the rice is sticky and fluffy. Comb it gently through with a fork to separate it a bit. Note: as a substitute for coconut milk – which is, in fact, water in the fresh state – buy some coconut cream and dilute it with water until you have a thin, milky white liquid. Make sure the rice has sufficient liquid to allow it to swell and cook properly. But if you do happen to have coconut palms in your garden, you will also need a highly educated monkey. On our way to Dungun market we had passed a man on a moped, with a smiling orange monkey sitting on the handlebars. I asked Awi what it was all about, and in one of life's curious reversals he told me they were both going to work, the monkey and the man, but the man was only the driver. The monkey was trained to scamper up the trees and throw down coconuts. So if you want to get ahead, get a monkey.

While the rice is cooking chop some batons of fresh pineapple and a few batons of cucumber and let them steep with finely chopped chilli in coconut vinegar. This side dish, a form of pickle like Indian chutneys and relishes, is known as a sambal.

And you will have a feast that is authentically Malay, typically Muslim and actually inexpensive and simple to prepare.

RENDANG AND OOMPH!

By the time we had packed up the gear and returned it to the store, it was half past three, and the hotel kitchen was shut. So we decided to drive along the coast to a small fishing village called Marang. It is a busy port but terribly difficult to enter because of a system of low-lying sandbanks at the mouth of the river. There is spectacular surf where the ocean hits the harbour entrance. Once boats are over the bar, every-thing is okay, because the harbour has deep water. The harbour is jammed with beautiful old wooden fishing boats painted in pale blues, lime greens, ochres and pinks, all with swept-up pointed bows designed to cope with the vagaries of the South China Sea.

We chose a food stall on the high road overlooking the port. Huge black storm clouds were rolling in eastwards from the sea. The café was a simple affair, a three-sided wooden shack, with a concrete floor and a crude kitchen out back, sheltered only by a piece of corrugated plastic for a roof. Half a dozen of those wonderful little bucket charcoal stoves, chipped and blackened, sat on two planks of wood, supported by two oil drums. There was a dirty looking fridge, cooled by an ancient, clacking compressor unit, sitting on bricks in a chicken-wire cage. And there were several smeared, chipped, pale Formica tables and an assortment of tubular steel chairs with ribbed leatherette seats. Another glass-fronted fridge, heavily choked with ice, contained root beer, Coke and fizzy soft drinks of alarming electric colours – Dayglo orange, nuclear red and Frankenstein green. There was a faded gold-painted Benson & Hedges display cabinet, empty except for a couple of packets of sweets and a few packs of American cigarettes. There were one or two garish religious prints, framed in peeling gilt, on the streaked, pale blue walls.

Thumbing through my guidebook earlier, I had learned that despite 'enthusiastic' logging, Malaysia is still rich in wildlife. I didn't have time to get into the jungle and see the elephants, tigers, wild pigs and the thousands of different species of birds, bees and butterflies, so I can't confirm the accuracy of the guide. But certainly the variety of wildlife in this little restaurant would have given David Attenborough many happy hours filming – bullfrogs croaked from under the fridge, lizards ran across the ceiling, tailless cats miaowed patiently under the table, butterflies danced in and out of the open front and birds – of slate-grey and brown with dashes of blue; they looked like small mynah birds – swooped on to the table and pecked away at the sugar bowl.

There were eight or nine of us altogether. Two ladies in traditional Muslim dress, with perfectly made-up faces, flashing eyes and happy smiles, came to talk to us and take our order. Between us we managed to string together a few requests; we knew that *Nasi Ayam* was pieces of roast chicken (served cold, tepid or hot depending on when the bird was cooked) dished up on a bed of crunchy lettuce, with a side dip of coconut vinegar, chopped chillies and shallots, and a beautifully lightly spiced chicken broth garnished with firm slices of spring onion. This came along with a bowl of coconut rice, garnished with finely chopped, crispy, deep-fried onion.

(Now, don't expect your food to be hot in these places. With the exception of the soups and noodle dishes, it will only be hot if it has just been cooked. Any kind of stew or curry will be cooked, placed in a large aluminium bowl and served until it has all gone. Then a new lot will be made, and if you happen to coincide with this you get it hot, if you come in three hours later you get it lukewarm.)

We knew that *Mee* meant egg or yellow noodles, so we said *Mee* and waved a lot, we said *Nasi Ayam* several times, we knew that fish was *Ikan*. By this time confusion and pandemonium had broken out. The ladies decided they could speak a little English, root beers were being served, I was pushed into the kitchen and shown a pot of a very dark meat curry, strongly tasting of aniseed. I discovered later that star anise is a favourite flavouring in this part of the world. I watched one of the women deftly bone a bream from the inside. She then oiled a piece of

sheet steel that was sitting on one of the charcoal stoves, placed a banana leaf on it, placed the fish on the banana leaf and covered it with a few scoops of red sauce. She placed a battered aluminium bowl over the fish and started to cook some noodles.

Grilling a piece of fish like that – or a whole fish – on a heated piece of sheet metal, is common in south-east Asia and really quite easy to do at home on the barbecue. The sauce was very simple: it was a load of chopped chillies, garlic, ginger and onion fried in oil. After they had been cooked to a golden brown, in went plenty of chopped peeled tomatoes, a lump of palm sugar and a small cube of fish paste, and you had the most wonderful sweet and sour tomato sauce. It was as easy as that.

Here in Malaysia they either serve noodles dry or wet. Dry ones are cooked noodles that have been strained from the water and simply stir-fried with absolutely anything you like. For example, if you have no meat or fish, then just as acceptable are a few chopped chillies, some ginger, some garlic, some little bits of onions and a few peas – and the same thing with shrimps or pieces of chicken or whatever you like.

Or they serve other noodles wet. And if they are wet noodles they will probably be flat ribbon ones. They will be cooked in chicken or fish stock, and garnished with sliced cabbage, spinach or Chinese leaves, bits of fish or shrimp or thin slivers of meat. Again, there are no rules, just principles.

This time the ladies brought us a wobbly, battered aluminium bowl of wet noodles – chicken stock with noodles, cabbage and squid. Then they produced the chicken and rice, the very dry-textured beef curry tasting of star anise, and deep-fried chicken drumsticks – tough and chewy but very tasty, cooked until they were almost black on the outside. There were sambals of pineapple and chillies and little dishes of fish sauce. There were small mackerel grilled until they were crispy and served with a spicy coconut sauce, simply made by frying a dollop of *rempah* and then mixing it with coconut milk and warming it through.

For thirty minutes we munched, chomped, slurped and chewed in a contented silence, interrupted only by the forty-eight-inch-screen colour television set which was showing Real Madrid playing some Eastern European country at football, with a hysterical Malaysian commentator shouting at the top of his voice.

It had grown quite dark; the owners switched on a couple of flickering neon tubes that bathed us in an eerie pale green light. And the storm was approaching fast. Some spectacular flashes of forked lightning preceded an awesome rolling thunderclap that Tim, who knows these things, later said lasted for a good thirty seconds. Then with a biblical roar, the wind ripped through the open back of the restaurant, snatching at paper napkins and cigarette butts. And then, as if God had pulled a mighty lever and released the trap, the rain fell, fast and furious, and smacked into the mud forecourt of the restaurant like half-inch lead shot, sending up little puffs of oxblood coloured dust, latticed with raindrops. Canvas awnings flapped and screamed, the wind howled, the thunder was moving westwards and the restaurant was suddenly full of refugees from the storm.

David was beside himself with excitement. 'That's it,' he cried, 'that's it, that's how we can do the final sequence.' (Today, by the way, was a Tuesday.)

'Tomorrow evening, Keith, we will set up on your balcony and we will film you cooking in the storm.'

For the next four nights, under the swaying palm trees on my balcony, we sat patiently in the suffocating heat, waiting for the rain that did not come.

Now, alert Reader, before I became carried away with the storm and the delightful feast – which, by the way, cost about £6 for eight or nine of us – I referred to a *rempah*. A *rempah* is one of the most important building blocks in Malaysian cookery. It is so important that prospective mothers-in-law, when judging the suitability of their sons' proposed brides, do so on their ability to make a good *rempah*.

In brief, it is a curry paste and in Malaysia, as in the United Kingdom, you can buy it ready-prepared in a jar. Or you can buy the ingredients and whizz them through your Magimix. Or, as in Malaysia, you can pick the ingredients from your own garden and grind them lovingly in a heavy stone pestle and mortar. And, indeed, every morning as we went to work, passing through the *kampongs*, young girls and grannies alike would sit, cross-legged, on a sheltered platform on stilts, patiently grinding away and chatting merrily.

The colour of a *rempah* can vary from a deep red to a dark yellow, depending on the emphasis you place on two particular ingredients. Red and very hot says chillies – dried red ones – while deep yellow means fewer chillies and more turmeric. Turmericky ones, to my mind, are better for white meat like chicken or pork (pork is, as I mentioned, not used in this part of Malaysia, but down in the south the Nonya people would use it) or with fish or shellfish.

For some Malays, a *rempah* – and they'd make a pound or so at a time so they could cook several meals with it – would be perhaps twenty-four small dried red peppers, ground to a smooth paste with half that quantity of finely chopped shallots and half that quantity again of chopped garlic, some finely chopped lemon grass and a tablespoonful of turmeric. And all this would be pounded and pounded until they had a smooth paste. For the yellow version they would decrease the volume of chillies and increase the volume of turmeric.

But if you want to go the whole nine yards and make up a jolly good jarful of the stuff to store in the refrigerator, you can take a couple of tablespoons of chopped fresh ginger, four lemon grass stalks, three or four whole cloves of garlic, a couple of tablespoons or more of peanuts, cashew nuts or almonds, half-a-dozen finely chopped shallots, thirty or forty small red chillies, a teaspoonful of ground black pepper and some salt.

Now, first chop everything into the finest possible dice and then – and don't let's be silly about this, don't reach for your pestle and

mortar, you will go mad in the process and, unless you have been doing this since you were about four years old, you won't get the required consistency – zap the lot into the food processor and whizz it until you have a thick red paste, and if it isn't red enough, add some more chillies. You must use this paste sparingly because it will be seriously hot.

I had to put this recipe to the test when I cooked for a Malay family in their own home. By the way, if you are travelling frequently in the East and you run the risk of going into people's houses don't, as I did on my first visit, wear 'Sanders of the River'-style lace-up leather boots. Instead wear any kind of slip-on shoe because shoes are forbidden in the homes.

The family lived in a simple wooden house on stilts; it comprised one room, partly divided by a piece of hardboard, which did not reach the ceiling and separated the family's sleeping quarters from the living area. It had electricity and a fan suspended from the ceiling spun slowly. There was a sideboard crudely made from bamboo, covered in photographs of the children taken at the various stages of religious inductions. One or two religious prints hung on the walls and the glass-fronted Formica cabinet contained a service of hideously decorated glass and cheap china tableware. There was a table and six chairs. And there was a leatherette G-plan-style sofa, a big chrome and glass occasional table and two woven plastic armchairs, one purple and one mauve. The floor was firstly covered in assorted offcuts of lino, the doormat was a beautifully laundered rice sack. Offcuts of a lurid cheap carpet were employed as rugs.

The kitchen, about eight feet long and four feet wide, was a rickety extension at the back. The floor was decked with hardwood, and through the slats you could see the family chickens scratching in the dust. There was a small round stainless steel sink, one tap, a two-burner gas ring. Shelves made from the untreated wood of fish or fruit boxes were covered with neatly folded newspaper. There was a scrupulously clean but chipped enamel plate rack, filled with assorted coloured plastic plates and bowls. There was a wok, some very light-weight aluminium saucepans, a selection of unmatched glasses, either gold-rimmed or with some sugar-frosted adornment. There was a simple Formica-topped kitchen table, on which folded newspapers had been carefully laid and which in turn were protected by a sheet of clear plastic.

As we set up the lights and Shaunagh prepared my ingredients, so the village became aware of our presence – through every window, through every crack in the wooden planks of the kitchen, and crowded in the living area, solemn, curious faces peered at us.

The idea was I would cook Beef Rendang for the family, the family would eat it and – as David explained to them in perfect English – they would chatter in a fruity, passionate and philosophical manner about Malaysian food. Needless to say they looked at him as if, and he is, stark raving bonkers. Our friendly translator of the day was one of the hotel receptionists, trained perfectly to utter sentences like 'We take Amex', 'The restaurant is there' and 'Have a nice day' – but fruity, passionate and philosophical was well beyond her capabilities.

So when she didn't understand what David was talking about, he turned to a small eight-year-old child and said: 'All the family must sit down and what you must do, my dear, is to go into the kitchen and bring the pot of Beef Rendang that Keith has cooked.' The little girl too, of course, didn't understand. I have encountered these situations so many times. They usually end up in a row between David and me because he accuses me of not pulling my weight and asking the right questions. And I have explained a dozen times there is no point in asking questions of people who a) don't understand you, b) can't speak your language and c) are wondering what the hell you are doing here in the first place.

And when we served them the food, they looked at it, they smiled shyly, they giggled, they spoke to each other, they all smiled at the camera – but would they eat it, would they heck! David was going potty because there would be no eating sequence to complete the cooking sequence. Everyone was sitting there, embarrassed and stony-faced. I suggested to David that he took the camera away and let them get on with it. And miraculously, the second the camera had gone and we were apparently no longer paying any attention to them, they started to eat with gusto, using their right hands.

Paul, who is very clever at this, had managed to reset the camera so they couldn't see it and was filming away happily without their knowledge when David, spotting a shiny and ornate aluminium teapot on the table, said, for better to see the food, 'Get that f . . . ing teapot off the f . . . ing table!'

Tim and Steve or somebody, obedient as ever, went to snatch it away. I managed to stop them just in time. 'It isn't a teapot, it is a ceremonial hand-washing vessel, and after you have finished eating the lady of the house rinses your fingers with it.' So the teapot stayed.

You will see the recipe for Beef Rendang that I used on this occasion on page 157. Mostly in Malaysia they would use buffalo meat; the hotel restaurants tend to use American tenderloin, but I would recommend some good quality stewing beef. It is important to remember that it should end up as a fairly dry curry that shouldn't swim in sauce. It is a hot dish and the pineapple and cucumber sambal helps to cool it down. It is also customary to serve it with coconut rice that is garnished with crispy fried chopped shallots or crispy fried pieces of dried anchovy or dried shrimp, and quartered hard-boiled eggs.

I ate Beef Rendang, or the chicken version of it, many times through-out my stay in Malaysia and often for breakfast, when it is usually served with a very spicy sambal made by frying shrimps with a little tomato sauce, onions and a dollop of *rempah* and fish paste.

Once the camera and the equipment had been packed away, the family neatly turned the tables on us. They produced a Beef Rendang and rice. Their Rendang was a much darker colour than mine, the meat was cooked 'till it was shredded – so it was shredded meat. And the rice, which was sticky and gooey, was fabulous – but it had been cooked in two-inch diameter bamboo tubes lined with palm leaves, moistened with coconut milk and propped like a set of mortars against a bar over an open fire. I ate theirs with relish, like you do with other people's cooking. And although I felt their rice was vastly superior to mine, I am not sorry to say my Rendang was better!

MAROONED

As the imams were calling the faithful to dawn prayers, the vans were loaded. And in the warm gloom, with a slowly rising sun just a faint glint behind the thick clouds, we set off again for Marang. On the roadside stalls charcoal stoves were flickering into life, shadowy figures shuffled around, rolling up blinds and setting out merchandise. The pathways between the *kampongs* underneath the coconut palms were filled with silhouetted figures shuffling off to the mosque.

We reached the port shortly after sunrise. The weekly market was in full swing. The road was steaming slightly as the morning sun dried the remains of a pre-dawn shower. Market traders, struggling with baskets filled with green-skinned oranges, stepped carefully over the corpse of a still-bleeding dog, recently run down by a motorbike.

We drove to the jetty and loaded the equipment on to two fishing boats that had been converted to carry passengers. They were the rough, wooden, high-prowed, graceful crafts we had seen the day before, painted in a variety of pale colours for practical rather than aesthetic reasons. Our boat had a long counter-stern with a teak cubicle about four feet high and four feet square. Inside the cubicle the deck was slatted. The captain and his mate sat on the high narrow bridge, towards the bow, and on the bridge aft the canvas sun blind was stretched on brightly painted, pitted steel tubes. Basic slatted benches, shiny from a fresh coat of paint, provided the passenger accommodation.

Once loaded up we set off, me standing like 'Sanders of the River', scanning the horizon with binoculars from the stern of my ship, the film crew and equipment in another boat. We hugged the edge of the harbour in a wide arc, where there was deep water, until we reached the harbour mouth where, as a result of the sand-bars, the breaking waves of the South China Sea created a two-hundred-yard deep and half-a-mile wide foaming hell of white water with waves that had teeth like bananas. The skipper slowed right down, lined the ship up with some point and, with a fierce thrust of the throttle, he accelerated through the foam like a javelin. Even at full power, from the albeit ancient and uncovered twin diesels, we took a hell of a pounding and, I thought, near-capsized more than once through that short stretch of turbulent water.

Once past that, we were into the steep swell of the ocean. The fishing boats, with their high bows and counter-sterns, steamed comfortably along. In a short time our destination, Capas Island, hove into view. Within an hour we were nudging against the stanchions of the long wooden jetty that protruded at right angles from the pure white sandy beach.

There was a small community of A-framed shacks along the beach. Behind that the island reared precipitously and was thickly clad in palms and bush. There was a small restaurant and bar, closed. And several signs prohibiting swimming, fishing, snorkelling and diving, which struck me as strange until we quickly discovered that, after all, it was a water sports resort, though described on the schedule as a totally uninhabited desert island. Presumably, the people who researched it – no names, no pack drill – couldn't have seen very much of the island from the bar in Marang, five miles away!

About a mile to the north, however, was another small island, and we borrowed a speedboat to check it out. It indeed was uninhabited; there were no buildings. So we decided to film there instead. The only trouble was, since there was no jetty, we had to transfer our equipment from the big ships to a small motorboat and ferry it to the island little by little. The schedule had said that the cooking sequence would be finished by noon. At twenty past one we lugged the final bit of gear ashore. I mention these details not out of malice or spite – I am certainly not complaining – it is just that most days our plans go awry.

By now it was burning hot and there was no shelter of any kind. A pair of black-headed sea eagles circled the peak of the mountainette that dominated the island. There were tall coconut palms where the beach gave way to the rocky interior. Half-an-hour's beachcombing yielded some oil drums and heavy wooden bleached fish boxes and we were able to create a pretty authentic Robinson Crusoe-style kitchen. We used palm leaves for a tablecloth.

Happily set up after the mishaps of the morning, we broke with our normal pattern of work and decided to have lunch before we filmed. After all, we were in no hurry because owing to the tide the boats couldn't take us off until six o'clock that evening!

There was a universal groan as we opened the stiff cardboard boxes containing the packed lunches provided by the hotel. Each had chicken and lettuce sandwiches made with rancid butter, stale-tasting chicken drumsticks and an orange. Had we had a fine-gauged throwing net we could have feasted on grilled anchovies. Within feet of the shore, in a foot or two of water, a massive shoal of them lay, black like the oil slick from a tanker disaster.

It grew hotter and the place was infested with flies, bees, wasps and mosquitoes. Gad, it was hell, I can tell you! I prepared a rather snazzy dish of fillets of fish poached in fresh coconut milk and served with a spicy coconut sauce. The recipe is on page 166.

In fact, the cooking sequence went very well. Paul had shot it from a tripod set up in the ocean and the filming was done and dusted except for some shots of me wandering around the beach or sitting on my fishing box in front of a fire like some dejected shipwrecked sailor. We just had three hours to sweat it out in the sun. In an attempt to amuse ourselves we did one of those Pythonesque sketches, 'What has a coconut ever done for us?' The answers were fairly obvious: you can eat it, you can drink it, you can eat from it or drink from it, you can

ME AND THE INCREDIBLE
FRYING MACHINE

SHAUNAGH FLOYD

STACKS OF *DIM SUM*
BAMBOO STEAMERS

WOODEN CARGO VESSELS
IN THE HARBOUR AT MALACCA

STEVE, PAUL, PRITCHARD, TIM

WITH THE GENERAL AT THE SNAKE FARM

THESE WERE NOT ON THE MENU

. . . THIS WAS!

MY NAME IS MOWGLI

SOMCHAI – OUR
CHEERFUL CHEF IN
NORTHERN THAILAND

MY CHUM CHOM
WITHOUT WHOM . . .

**IN MALACCA, I WAS
ONLY DREAMING**

**ONE OF THE
COLOURFUL MARKETS**

**LISU HILL TRIBE
CHILDREN**

build with it, you can make matting from it, you can roof a hut with the leaves of it, etc., etc.

After twenty minutes this inevitably palled, and a desultory splash in the deep sea did little to lift our spirits. We mooched disconsolately up and down the blasted beach or occasionally sat uncomfortably on a blazingly hot rock. Finally, our boats, preceded by the motor launch, hove into view. And a wild cheer went up from the desperate band of shipwrecked city dwellers, who were practically at the end of their tethers after just seven hours on a desert island. The worst thing of all was that someone had left the lid off the polystyrene box of iced beer, and towards the end we had been obliged to sip tepid Tiger lager.

It was almost dusk as we entered the harbour and like most nights we just made it to the little café as the storm, which had been gathering for an hour, broke. David was furious. Every night at six o'clock there was a spectacular downpour, except on the evenings we were set up on the balcony of my log cabin, ready to film it.

Across the street from the café or the shack, small naked children danced gleefully in the rain. Mothers emerged and rubbed shampoo into their hair, which the rain quickly rinsed out. The night was growing very dark now. The floor of the coffee stall was inches deep in water, and the Formica tabletops were awash with drips coming through the leaking corrugated roof. The atmosphere was jolly; the coffee was thick and sweet with condensed milk.

All of a sudden, the chattering stopped and, except for the drumming of the rain on the roof, the place fell expectantly silent. Splashing through the puddles came four men, their thin cotton working clothes drenched to the skin, carrying a long palm mat, rolled up like a stretcher. They placed the bundle on the longest table, underneath the swinging tinny lamp, and folded back the mat – to reveal the dead body of a boy, aged about twelve, who had been swept overboard a fishing vessel during the previous day's storm.

MALACCA (MELAKA)

After the sleepy *kampongs* of north-east Malaysia, where the rhythm of life is largely dictated by the weather, the tide and the call to prayers, the bustling, noisy town of Malacca, its streets chock-a-block with impatient drivers honking their horns, came as a shock. But it was good to check into a hotel, the Ramada Renaissance, that had all the bits a film crew on the road need – twenty-four-hour room service, telephones, televisions and minibars, a coffee shop open round the clock (as a useful alternative to the more formal restaurant) – and for me, joy of joy, endless supplies of hot water.

In the fourteenth century Malacca, strategically placed in the Straits, became an important trade centre as the Chinese and then the Indians came to buy and sell. In the sixteenth century the Portuguese arrived, hungry for spices and gold. From the latter half of the seventeenth century to the middle of the nineteenth, the Dutch dominated the region, trading in silk and porcelain, camphor, sandalwood and tin. In the mid-1800s the French defeated the Dutch. Following treaties with France, the British took over Malacca and the Straits and indeed all of the former Dutch colonies. But by about 1830, the once crowded international trading port of Malacca had silted up and trade declined.

Malacca was a racially tolerant place and mixed marriages between the Chinese and the Malays produced the wealthy aristocratic class known as the Peranakans. And they fitted readily and comfortably into the British colonial way of life. (There is also a big Peranakan commune in Penang.) They were known as the Queen's (Victoria) Chinese. They wore spectacular clothes, played bridge, drank Cognac, and evolved an exquisite blend of Chinese and Malay food known as Nonya – although you'd need to be born in Malacca to distinguish *easily* between

Malay and Nonya because like the Nonya cooks, the food is inter-married too.

In Chinatown there are one or two Peranakan merchants' houses, lovingly maintained from the Victorian era, crammed with black Malacca wooden furniture encrusted with mother of pearl. Indeed, around the river there is ample architectural evidence of the previous occupying powers. There is a Portuguese fort, there are brilliant Chinese merchants' town houses, Dutch administrative buildings and houses, and Catholic and C of E churches, and terrific stucco Chinese shop houses. Malacca also boasts the biggest and oldest Chinese cemetery outside of China itself. It has the oldest Hindu temple in Malaysia, the oldest mosque, the oldest church and the oldest Chinese temple.

Chinatown, with its shop houses busy repairing bikes, making tin trunks or selling Buddhas with incense, is a fascinating place to stroll around. There are great antique shops, dozens of street hawkers cooking noodles and rice and, of course, the ubiquitous satay – which isn't Malaysian at all; its origins are Arab.

Stroll down to the harbour and you will see, as Conrad saw, ancient Indonesian-style boats unloading wood and copra. These ships, between sixty and a hundred and twenty feet in length, have no engines. Crew accommodation is a plain hut built on the stern. Forward of these crude cabins there is an unprotected galley on the deck. A galley is a couple of the terracotta charcoal stoves, alongside which is a cage filled with rabbits or chickens. Today Malaysia is a fast developing country, becoming more prosperous by the day. But by nature the Malaysians prefer farming and fishing to the brutality of commerce. Consequently, it is the Chinese who are the driving commercial force.

Anyway, back to the food. I don't want you to have the wrong impression, but alcohol is pretty difficult to come by, especially in eastern Malaysia. And we were delighted to find, after two weeks of drinking passion-fruit juice and lime juice, that the bar of our hotel didn't charge like a wounded buffalo for its spirits. So we decided on this, our first night, to celebrate a good week's filming. In the bar they were playing beautifully outdated Western popular music like 'The Tennessee Waltz' and 'Pickin' A Chicken With Me' – you know, all those people like Teresa Brewer and Hank Williams. And before we knew where we were, we were happily buying round after round.

Morning brought a collection of sore heads to the coffee shop for breakfast. There was a long buffet of European and Asian food, a huge variety of fruit juices, fresh fruit, pastries, hams and cheeses – it really was superb. By the way, don't have bacon in these places because it is not made from pigs but from beef and it is dreadful.

However, I needed something to clear my head and in one of the stainless steel pots was a rich red Chicken Rendang. And at 7.15 a.m. along with some boiled rice, prawn sambal and extra chillies, I tucked in. Never again will I have croissants and orange juice or eggs and bacon. Give me Chicken Rendang for breakfast every time! Some mornings, for a change, I had a plate of simple fried noodles with chillies, shrimps and chopped spring onions, with a spoonful of the prawn sambal.

One of the great dishes of this region is called *Laksa*. There are street hawkers all over the town, selling it from little kitchens built on the back of mopeds and bicycles. Basically, it is a spicy coconut soup filled with noodles and pieces of chicken or shrimp. I had eaten it before in Singapore and in Australia, but people kept telling me that it was in Malacca where I would find the genuine article. And I did. Although others claim it to be a Filipino dish.

During the course of my research, talking to cooks and reading recipes, it became evident that there is much more to a *Laksa* than meets the eye. There are many interpretations of the dish and I was genuinely anxious when, in the borrowed kitchen of the house of one of Malacca's most important citizens and under the scrutiny of the ladies of the house, I began to prepare it.

The variety of ingredients alone is daunting. Rice noodles, chillies, garlic, coriander, cumin, shrimp paste, onions, peanut oil, coconut milk, sugar, chicken, beansprouts, beancurd, spring onions, shrimps – but once you come to grips with it and divide it into a simple step-by-step procedure, it is quite a straightforward dish. But you must allow at least an hour to prepare it, even though it only takes about ten minutes to assemble and serve. The recipe is on page 178.

But here are a few tips. First, prepare your curry paste, your *rempah*, and put it to one side. Then fry in peanut oil some chopped, boned and skinless chicken, and put that aside. Then fry your cubes of pressed beancurd until they are golden and crunchy on the outside. Next fry some sliced onion until it is golden brown and crispy and set aside. If you do those things first and then, and only then, lay out your ingredients on the kitchen table in the order in which you are going to use them, can you proceed with confidence.

My *Laksa* prepared, I offered it to the family as usual, and to my utter joy and Pritchard's unexpressed delight, they tucked into it with gusto. 'You have just the right blend of sweet and sour in the sauce, the shrimps [I had added shrimps] are not overcooked, the chicken is perfect.' And so it went on. It even more than made up for the disappointment I was still harbouring from my failure to excite the family I had cooked the Beef Rendang for.

But if you find *Laksa* all too difficult, another Malacca speciality, which is very simple to prepare, is called *Nasi Lemak* – which means rice cooked in coconut milk, *Nasi* being rice. Simply, as I have described elsewhere in the book, cook some short-grain, well-washed rice in coconut milk, which you season with, say, three pandan leaves, which you have knotted together to bruise them. But as you probably won't be able to find pandan leaves in Nempnet Thubwell, you can use vanilla pods instead, the flavour is very similar. The rice is fluffy, slightly sticky and sweet. Serve it with some hard-boiled eggs cut into quarters, fried peanuts – that's fresh peanuts by the way, and remember to take off the shells and skins first – and also with a little fish sambal.

To make this tasty sambal, first pound together a handful of chillies and shallots, a few Brazil or macadamia nuts and a dollop of fish sauce. Then remove the heads and the nasty bits from inside your fresh anchovies (or you could use dried shrimps), heat a little oil and fry them until they are a lovely crispy brown. Lift them out and put on one side.

Now fry your paste in the same oil for a couple of minutes. Add a dash of tamarind juice, season with a pinch of salt and some sugar, and simmer gently until the sauce is thick. Stir in the fried anchovies and it's ready. Delicious!

We spent the next couple of days bobbing about on fishing boats, visiting rubber plantations, cooking Chilli Crabs and eating Chinese street food. Hafiz and Awi were darting about making things happen – hiring jeeps, borrowing speedboats, rearranging schedules – in short, just doing what the Malaysians are really good at, being kind, friendly, generous and helpful. We all wished we could stay another week instead of having to go to Hong Kong.

At the farewell party in a smart Chinese restaurant Hafiz – after seconds of soul-searching – could see no good reason why, as a Muslim, he could not accept a farewell present of (among other things) a large bottle of Johnny Walker Black Label whisky.

HONG KONG

'Hong Kong – A borrowed place living on borrowed time'
The Times, 5 March 1981

The first-class departure lounge at Hong Kong airport was virtually empty and, after pacing up and down a few times and sipping at a free beer, I left the lounge to look for the rest of the crew, whom I knew had run into complications trying to get their large amount of equipment checked in. I found them in one of the public bars, frustrated and angry that despite having business-class tickets and having paid £1000 excess baggage charge, they had been refused invitations to the lounge. It was a sad but somewhat apt summing-up of the attitude of the place. And, quite frankly, it was a relief to be moving on from Hong Kong, this time to South Vietnam, to Saigon – formerly the Paris of the East, now Ho Chi Minh City.

To kill time, as you so often do on trips like these, we decided to have some lunch at the airport – even though we had had a wonderful farewell breakfast at the Mandarin Hotel. Now that was a good part of

Hong Kong. I had been doing a bit of research into airport eating and was thinking perhaps Hong Kong could redeem itself with a cheap and excellent meal. But in Hong Kong, of all places, the self-service restaurant owed more to an Australian outback Chinese takeaway than to what was supposed to be the culinary jewel of the East.

Afterwards, we still had an hour or two before we could board the plane and I tried to focus my thoughts on the last seven days spent in Hong Kong. But at this moment, the only image of it I had was of the hundreds of Filipino women sitting around the square behind the Mandarin on Sunday morning, clutching their possessions in brightly coloured polythene bags, swapping clothes, massaging each other, chattering, doing their hair, their fingernails, sharing food parcels, sharing drinks, singing, praying, laughing, crying, holding out bags with 'Love Offering' printed on them – a gentle, sad way of begging.

'Why are they there?' I had asked.

'Oh, they just like to meet their own people on their day off.'

The reality of it was that on their days off these nurses and nannies, cooks, stewardesses, cleaners and waitresses were required to leave the house of their employ for the entire day.

There must have been more to Hong Kong than that. I am sure there was. But it is always difficult at the end of a frantic week to focus on a place, and a week is hardly long enough, even though we did get a little bit under the skin of this extraordinary – what is it, a city, an island, a massive shopping centre? If you haven't been to Hong Kong and you can't afford to go, take a trip to Jersey or Guernsey. And walk past the duty free stores, designer clothes shops, watch shops, and the banks and insurance offices, change the signs over the doors into Chinese characters – and you have Hong Kong on a small scale.

I think the only thing I liked about Hong Kong, I said to myself while I was sitting in the airport, was seeing all the tower blocks lit up at night and watching the jumbo jets coming in to land below the high-rise skyline. When we had come into Hong Kong I had been on the flight deck. The approach was both frightening and spectacular. The illuminated high-rise buildings were like the silver and gold teeth of a massive dragon's mouth. And the plane flew straight into it.

HONG KONG JOTTINGS

To kill time while I was waiting for our flight to Saigon to be called I jotted some notes of things I had seen in Hong Kong, which I thought would give a particular flavour of the place when I came to write this book. Here they are.

Expats and Steak at the Mandarin

When we arrived we had been greeted like royalty by the manager of the Mandarin Oriental Hotel and shown to a luxurious suite on the seventeenth floor. It had a spectacular view of the harbour, busy with yellow and black tugs, green and white ferries, grey naval and police boats, little varnished sampans with yellow canopies, rusty freighters, container ships painted in brilliant blue, craft of all kind churning up and down the restless water, gantries and cranes, wharfs covered in rubber tyres. There were junks rushing by laden with vegetables and hardware goods, fishing boats going in and out. The sampans and junks were fantastic; they were like nautical Dodgem cars, driven by elderly ladies or men, ferrying passengers and merchandise. Food was even being cooked on these little junks, to be delivered boat to boat – like floating kitchens. And, of course, there were the mountains and the very tall high-rise blocks surrounding the harbour – Aberdeen Harbour. Fascinating.

It had taken sixteen hours to travel from Malacca to this haven of self-indulgence … On the top floor of the hotel there was a superb marble caviar bar, an elegant French restaurant and a fine Chinese restaurant. But the grill room was more to my liking – it had a wonderful green lacquered sideboard and benches and cupboards with brass strips in relief. Comfortable armchairs to sit in, excellent Chinese murals in soft and subdued fawns, browns, rusts, ochres and reds. We had a back-to-the-womb dinner of grilled steak, green salad, cheese and a superb almond and ginger ice cream, washed down with a bottle of Morgon. We relaxed with espresso coffee and Armagnac and retired to bed for a good night's sleep in an emperor-sized bed, too tired and too content with this luxury to feel the pain of the restaurant's bill, just over £200.

After breakfast the next day, observational shots in Maxim's Palace *dim sum* restaurant. Lurid red, rectangular dining area the size of a rugby pitch ... spectacular, stainless steel, long and narrow kitchen with a gigantic gas range snorting flames and hissing steam like an army of Chinese dragons. An army of white-clad chefs furiously preparing ten thousand baskets of *dim sum* a day, from over one hundred and fifty choices. It was the most impressive culinary experience I had in Hong Kong, apart from that at the long-established mock Tudor-style Jimmy's Kitchen Restaurant, which is considered totally passé by the languid, long-serving, stir-crazy Brits. I found its old-fashioned mix of English colonial curries and corned beef and cabbage an amusing diversion.

I think, though, you can get just as good Chinese food in Manchester or Gerrard Street ...

It was 7 o'clock in the evening in the Captain's Bar, which was full of the self-styled, wise-cracking elite of the international business traveller, selling each other things that neither one possesses ...

■ 'For just 2.5 million US I can have this in Saudi by the 30th.'

■ 'Once the Governor approves it, and Henry assures me he will ... it's in the bag, old boy.'

■ Behind us an Englishman of about thirty-five years, who must have been a role-model for many of Simon Raven's characters, was lackadaisically signing up a bemused Chinese couple into a Hong Kong franchise to pyramid-sell slimming aids, a shocking example of the toothless lion that appears to be the British trade thirst in the East.

■ A Texan barged between my wife and me to say 'Hi, I'm Ed, caught your show on the World Service last night, it's funny.'

'Thank you very much.'

Then in the way that only Americans can do, in a series of rapid-fire sentences beginning 'I am away from home a lot, but my wife and I are happily married – she's happy and I'm married', he continued to unload an unasked-for potted history of his life in two minutes.

■ Smart lady in business suit, earnestly talking stocks and shares in her capacity as a trouble-shooting roving accountant for an Australian-based multinational company, and conning drinks from the two Lancashire businessmen who were sitting either side of her. She had them like a spider has a fly, except that they were too drunk to notice and too obsessed with this 'accountant's' cleavage.

■ A Brit in a well-cut suit and tie, which could have been mistaken for a Brigade one, and presumably often is, his hair still wet from the shower he has taken after the evening's game of squash, volunteered as he squeezed into the crowded bar, 'Don't move; staying at the Mandarin? Of course, most of these fellows stay in rooming-houses in Kowloon and just come here to do their deals. I say, have you been to Bentley's Oyster Bar yet? A pal of mine runs it, only place to eat in Hong Kong.'

■ A lugubrious Welsh voice whispered in my ear, 'Don't they talk bullshit!' I look up to find a well-built man in a leather jerkin, half-rimmed spectacles, with a loosened tie and an open-necked shirt.

'Thomas, Terry Thomas is the name,' holding out his hand. 'I know who you are so I shan't embarrass you with that crap, but would you and your wife like a drink?'

We had been in the bar for about an hour and of the twenty or so people who had foisted themselves into our conversation, he was the first to introduce himself and offer a drink. It seemed that Terry was the head of a Bangor University team that trundles around the Third World helping to save rainforests.

'It's dead simple,' he said, 'first you build a buffer around the endangered forests, a buffer of rubber trees, carefully placed so that when they've taken, you then plant pineapples in between the rows of rubber trees. Then after three years, in between both of those you plant banana trees. Then, underneath all of them, when they've really grown, you plant rattan palms so you can make chairs out of them – the rattan trees are shade-tolerant – so you've got cash crops in rubber, in pineapples and bananas and a building material out of rattan, a construction material. This satisfies the desire of the farmers to make their money and at the same time enables them to leave the forests alone.'

In point of fact, in between several of the Mandarin's splendid and expensive beers, Terry took a couple of hours to explain this. But I have simply attempted here to hone it to the nub of essential information, in case any of you want to dash out to Malaysia, South America or somewhere and help...

■ A group of three Brits, evidently time-serving Hong Kong residents, were betting serious money on the precise time of arrival of the fourth member of their evening drinking school. Bets placed, they reviewed the day's racing at Hong Kong's Happy Valley, and drifted on to discuss the forthcoming yacht club ball.

In Excess

Thus my week in Hong Kong passed, days spent sitting in traffic jams in cars where smoking was not permitted but the driver was allowed a mobile phone, a CB set and a taxi radio network – and used all three at the same time.

Printed on the side of one bus was 'Seating Upstairs 69', 'Seating Downstairs 40' – that's 109. And 'Standing 34'. That's over 140 passengers on a double-decker bus. Ridiculous. And I remember the odd little gem like Ice House Street, a lovely name. I wonder if it will still be called that in a couple of years.

Foreign Correspondents' Club

To try and get some feel of the place, to try and get some impressions from people who weren't there just to trade shares or buy money, we went to the Foreign Correspondents' Club. I don't think I saw any foreign correspondents. But I did overhear two spruce Americans, in their early thirties, wondering and worrying how they could rearrange their flight from Hong Kong to Malaysia now that they had discovered their present flight took them over Vietnam. Such intrepid travellers. Don't the Americans know, hasn't anyone told them, that the War ended twenty years ago?

We walked back from the Correspondents' Club to the hotel, with dragons and firecrackers on every street corner, but, frankly, it is more fun dancing round the Hobby Horse Floral Dance at Padstow!

Bored to Shop

Hong Kong is supposed to be a great shopping centre, they all tell you before you go out there. You can get anything there. You can get suits made. But shopping in Hong Kong is the most infuriating thing in the world.

'Good morning. I would like a pair of these shoes in size 43.'

'Yes, sir. Please sit down for a moment and I will get them for you.'

Ten minutes later the assistant returns with a pair of shoes. 'Here we are, sir.'

Before your big toe is halfway down you know your foot won't fit, you look at the other shoe. 'But these are size 42.'

'Yes, sir.'

'But they don't fit.'

'Ah! How about a jacket – would you like a jacket?'

'Have you no shoes in size 43?'

'Yes, sir,' he says, indicating a pair of terrible white suede monstrosities with red laces and metal buckles. 'How about some shirts instead?'

'No, I have plenty of shirts, thank you.'

They just won't let you go. I spent a week trying to buy a lens for my camera and yet Hong Kong is full of camera shops! But they just didn't have a prime 35mm lens in Hong Kong.

'Good morning. Do you have a 35mm lens for my Canon camera?'

'Yes, of course. Please sit down.' You sit down, you light a cigarette and they give you an ashtray. The assistant spends ten minutes punching a computer and then rummaging through drawers and shelves only to say he hasn't one. 'But I do have a 35mm to 70mm telescopic lens.'

'I don't want that.'

'Well, you should have that because that way you can use it on 35, 50 and 70mm.'

'I don't want that, I already have one.' (And Paul the cameraman has told me that if I have a prime lens and use 400 films I will take much better pictures.)

'Would you like a 50mm?'

'No, I want a 35mm. I have already explained why.'

'Well, I can order you one. It will be here tomorrow.'

'Could you develop these films for me?'

'Yes, they will be back in two hours.'

But they are not back two days later. They will try and sell you anything. It goes on and on and on.

Cigarettes are £3 a packet.

There are endless shopping malls and banks and where there are little shops – if they were in Malaysia they would be artisanal, entrepreneurial Aladdin's caves making what they sold or small workshops replacing valves or grinding engines – here they are full of gimcrack touristy things like gilt frames, cheap silver statues, plastic crap.

Sweet and Sour

Still sitting in the airport departure lounge, the more I thought about my sojourn in Hong Kong, the more depressed I became. In the New Territories, for instance, we had found a delightful fishing village, Sai Kung, a harbour crammed with water boats ferrying everything from television sets to passengers – and it was wonderful. The atmosphere was electric, and porters pushed trolleys piled high with wicker baskets full of gleaming fish, people were chattering, buying and selling.

We had asked our interpreter from the Hong Kong Tourist Board, a pleasant young man called Cecil, to obtain permission for us to film. It was refused. We had never, in the seven or eight years of making these programmes, been refused permission to film, anywhere. We were all amazed. And filming market scenes before the cooking sequences is an important part of the make-up of the programme. Finally, somebody gave permission. We bought our fish and set up the portable wok at the end of the jetty, having taken great care to keep out of the way of the odd porter who trundled by, or the odd passenger climbing on to the ferries – brightly painted sampans with coloured awnings and driven by decorative gnarled old ladies, not one under the age of eighty.

Suddenly there was a crowd around us as there usually is, often curious, often amused, often surprised and frequently amazed by this motley clan of Brits who stand there gesticulating and stirring things in frying pans. But this crowd was hostile, they wanted money. But they had no right to ask for money. As we started to film and the arguments grew louder, the ringleader took off his jacket and held it in front of the camera, like a cockerel in a farmyard protecting his territory – and this man was impotent with rage.

We told the tourist guide to sort out the crowd, but he was no match for this wily old gangster. It was here I did one of these pieces to camera which I hope to God will never be shown, on which I vented a whole lot of anti-Chinese feelings. We had come, of course, to praise the place not to bury it.

However, we filmed on and I cooked a wonderful dish with a sweet and sour sauce and fried prawns, and all the while this man was clenching his fists and gesturing like a bully looking for a fight, scream-ing and shouting. This was our first day's filming in Hong Kong. What a welcome, I thought. The man strutted and postured. Flapping his coat like a cockerel flaps his wings when threatened. The crowd were behind him. Pointing at us and nodding their heads each time he screamed abuse.

'Get that ... tourist guide to sort him out,' I shouted.

'He can't, he doesn't speak their dialect.' Some guide!

It was a ridiculous scene. On my little portable table I had a mountain of tiger prawns, a bowl of red peppers, a basket of red chillies, bottles of sweet and sour sauce, red and glistening bottles of rice wine, a bowl of sugar, sesame oil, water, pepper and salt – all beautifully arranged as if we were taking a studio packshot for the front cover of a book. The wok was roaring away, the backdrop was epic – fishing nets and rickety, iron-roofed warehouses, shabby apartments covered in washing. In front little sampans gathered round in a circle, their engines idled noisily. David was getting more and more and more angry and finally we decided, 'To hell with it, let's go.'

I dredged the prawns in seasoned flour, deep-fried them in hot oil, drained them, ditched most of the oil, next chopped vehemently at the peppers and chillies and threw them in. I added rice wine and sweet and sour sauce, then I added the seasoning and thickened it with a little bit of mixed cornflour and water.

I tossed in the prawns, stirred them around for a few seconds. I was talking with a rapidity that surprised even me; and if you see the scene on television: NO, I'm not pissed, just fired up by a bunch of shits.

I dished it up to a lady who had been silent amid this hostile crowd. For a few seconds she shied away, then she took one, bit it and smiled. The disgruntled man with the jacket climbed into his sampan defiantly – still demanding money – but he HAD to go, he had cus- tomers. And that's money too!

Curiously, against the run of play, when I later saw the rushes of the programme we had shot, Hong Kong seems to be an exciting place. But for me, I'd rather do a week's community service at the Metro Centre in Newcastle! But if you do have to stay in Hong Kong, check into the Mandarin and don't leave 'till it's time to catch your flight out.

JOURNEY TO SAIGON

Finally, the flight was called and in the suffocating heat, after a jerky bus ride when we were threatened with being wiped out by jets landing every two or three seconds, we shuffled on to the Cathay Pacific 747 – or whatever it was. And to make matters worse it was a 'No Smoking' flight.

None of us could decide how long the flight was going to be. David was still operating on Devon time. No one could be certain if there was now eight or nine hours' time difference from the UK. At any rate it promised to be at least two hours so I decided to pass the journey reading Conrad – something I had been trying to do for the last four weeks but for some reason or another had failed to get round to it. So as a short cut I thought I would read Gavin Young's Odyssey to find out who Conrad really was. I also had Graham Greene and Somerset Maugham to read (so I could make witty asides in my pieces to camera). But oh dear! Conrad's heavy, this whole effort was now getting out of hand. David had the idea that *Heart of Darkness* or *Lord Jim* would be some kind of coathanger on which to hang our trip. He was for ever saying, 'I bet Conrad would have seen that', 'I bet Conrad was there'. But he wasn't reading his books either.

The plane took off. I watched the office and apartment blocks give way to a ridge of mountains, to a turquoise sea – and Hong Kong was gone.

The stewardess brought us some drinks and another dish of those dreadful sweet, spicy, stale, crackly, multicoloured rice balls, which I can't stand. But I always pick one up and spit it out. Soon they would serve a meal. I reached for my guidebook and flipped through.

'... Ho Chi Minh (he who enlightens). The great revolutionary came from a poor but aristocratic family. About 1910, under an assumed name, he left the country on the French ship *Amiral Latouch-Treville*. Before ending up in Paris, he travelled to America, England, and South Africa. And it was in Paris, under the influence of the French communist party newspaper *L'Humanité*, that he was converted to communism.

In 1923 he left France for Moscow, where he was trained as a spy. In 1930 he formed the Vietnamese communist party, whose main objective was probably to get rid of the French, but ultimately resulted in the débâcle which was the Vietnam War.

He was apparently a well-liked and charismatic man. But much more important to us and not known by many, he worked as a pastry chef under the legendary Escoffier at the Carlton Hotel in London...'

I heard a succession of ding-dongs from the cabin and I knew at any moment the stewardess would announce our imminent descent into Saigon. Before I land, here are my thoughts on Vietnamese food:

Some Notes on Vietnamese Cooking

■ Vietnamese cooking has been influenced for two thousand years by the Chinese, and since the nineteenth century by the French.

■ Mongolian invasions of Vietnam in the thirteenth century made a big impression on their food too, in the form of steamboats or Mongolian hotpots. A lasting example of this is the classic and wonderful breakfast dish called *Pho* (pronounced fir), a beef and noodle soup.

■ Other influences – Laos, Cambodia and Thailand – have added a spiciness to Vietnamese cooking because these countries have all been under the cultural influence of India at some time or another. Hence curry dishes and Indian spices have rubbed off into Vietnamese cooking.

■ Then in the sixteenth century, after the discovery of the New World, European traders introduced potatoes, peanuts, tomatoes and corn.

■ But despite all these culinary influences Vietnam has remained fiercely independent, taking the best of them, but maintaining its own distinctive style. For example, at first sight much Vietnamese food looks Chinese, but at first taste you realise it is so much lighter, so much more flavoursome, so much more interesting. And the Vietnamese don't use cornflour, monosodium glutamate or artificial flavourings. They like their food very simple.

The generous use of herbs, such as lemon grass, dill, mint, coriander and basil, and the habit of wrapping delicate spring rolls in leaves (maybe spinach or lettuce) sets Vietnamese cooking apart from its neighbours. Speaking of green leaves and vegetables: Another distinctive feature of Vietnamese cooking is the mighty fish sauce (*nuoc mam*). And though it is used in the way the Chinese or Japanese use soy sauce, mainly as a dipping sauce, it is made from salted anchovies that are layered together in barrels and allowed to ferment, after which the liquid is strained off and bottled. Often this is seasoned or flavoured further with lemon juice, chillies or chopped shallots. Every cook has his own way of doing *nuoc mam* sauce.

If you are a non-meat-eater, many Vietnamese dishes can be adapted to suit your tastes. For example, substitute pak choy or other Asian greens for meat in soups and *phos*. Or with spring rolls or stuffed lettuce rolls, for instance, you can always use sweetcorn and/or mushrooms instead of meat or fish.

■ The Vietnamese enjoy stir-frying but use very little oil. And when oil is called for, they usually use vegetable oil; they are very health-conscious. They love steaming, but, above all, it is the often charcoal-fired steamboats that are employed to produce a wonderful range of soups and stews. They eat with chopsticks, and with Chinese soup spoons. And as a result of the French occupation, they make splendid bread.

■ Rice is the staple part of any meal; it is nearly always served in noodle form.

■ If you are going to get into Vietnamese cooking it would be fun to buy all the toys, like steamboats, chopsticks, wok, little bowls and wire strainers to lift things out of the steamboats. Establish a good delicatessen where you can buy your fish sauce, a greengrocer where you can get your fresh herbs.

And have fun!

VIETNAM

SAIGON

Below it was very green, of so many shades there aren't enough adjectives in the English language to describe them, rich red earth ploughed (invariably by hand) to create plots of vegetables, rice paddies. The airport was in sight. A long, long, desolate strip with a cluster of single-storey buildings at the far end. It had the air of one of those disused RAF airfields you find in Kent, except the runway had been lengthened some time back to accommodate the B52 bombers.

Saigon airport is a shabby building painted in institutional creams and greens. There was no air-conditioning and no apparent bar. It was stiflingly hot. We were given forms to fill in that required us to list every item of personal belonging we were bringing into Vietnam – watches, cameras, cigarettes, clothes, jewellery. I have never spent so long getting into a country: for two hours they rummaged through our trunks and flipped through my cookery books to make sure they weren't pornographic. The crew's videos were counted and recounted.

And it was becoming hotter, stickier and darker outside and we were feeling more and more and more uncomfortable. Time dragged as they took yet another piece of equipment away to analyse it, and the cameraman Paul panicked that they would put the tapes through some sort of infrared machine that would wipe off what we had done. And yet in contrast to this heavy hand of authority, from fear of smuggling and reselling our goods, the military officials who dealt with us – the customs officers, the police, the military police (all in neatly pressed olive-green drill suits) – were utterly charming, and told us not to worry that it was taking so long. We didn't understand their language, but that was the impression they gave us. It was the first time we had seen genuine smiles and heard real laughter in a week.

It was quite dark and raining when we finally got into a battered limousine that took us down the long straight wide road into town. There was a blustery, hot wind fighting for attention with short, heavy down-pours of warm rain. The clack of erratic windscreen wipers – one with no rubber so I couldn't see through the windscreen – was nerve-racking. And the constant hooting of a truck behind us was head-splitting. And yet despite the massive, two-wheeled army of scooters and cyclos taking workers home, there was a wonderful sense of excitement. There were no neon advertising signs, no traffic lights, no lane discipline. There wasn't that manic under-roar of motorised traffic that drums in your ears in most major cities. Just a swish of tyres and the honking of horns.

Amid this mechanical millrace, weaving in and out on their mopeds, were straight-backed pretty girls in miniskirts, their hands and nail varnish protected by long white gloves, spindly old men peddling heavy loads, proud families – father, two children and mother – sitting primly on their mopeds. Laughing boys in baseball caps, seven to a moped, were trying to race their friends home. Now and again a low-watted light bulb swinging on a piece of flex illuminated crowded stalls made from palm and canvas. In an eerie flicker you caught a glimpse of charcoal braziers, of women treading Singer sewing machines and men working lathes, children playing and old men staring. I wound down the window to smell the soft scent of this night's breeze. The sky was deep purple and there was a shadowy pink gloom over Saigon.

'. . . AND IS THERE COBRA STILL FOR TEA?'

The fat, grey, oily waters of the Saigon River glided through the mono-chromatic green patchwork quilt of vegetable plots, paddy fields and oil palms. This river – a massive, mythical python – oozed with power and an inscrutable sense of purpose, as it slid through this fertile alluvial plain to the South China Sea.

From my air-conditioned room in the Saigon Floating Hotel, the view was totally absorbing. Across the wide river, there were tin-roofed warehouses and bamboo shacks – simple dwellings built on stilts where the river people live and work. Upstream, there were enormous old grey cranes poking into the sky. The tatty cranes, rusting warehouses and derelict slipways gave way eventually to the voracious Vietnamese vegetation, bamboo, palms and coconut trees.

To the left, there were ships being repaired in dry dock. Gangs of men sitting on planks, suspended by ropes from the deck, were chip-ping away rusting, flaking paint with hammers. They wore only shorts and pointed straw hats. They were wiry and tough and were working with manic energy. They were wearing no shoes.

Unpainted, faded, grey wooden junks, so heavily laden with coco-nuts their gunnels were all but awash, made their way like submerged crocodiles in endless procession to the side of a dirty freighter – high-prowed and with a rounded counter-stern, a ship from another era, a ship once black, white and red that would have been familiar to Somer-set Maugham or Graham Greene. The wooden junks, their high and aft cabins strewn with multicoloured laundry left out to dry, were delivering coconuts to the freighter. The air was still; it was choking with humidity, and the big red flag with the yellow star drooped lifelessly from the peeling white flagpole astern. They were hand-loading coconuts into the cavernous belly of this battered old ship.

Two noisy passenger ferries – crowded with people, animals, children and bicycles – chugged and clattered endlessly across the river and back. Long-tailed boats laden with shiny, glistening earthenware rain barrels roared up and down the river. Those who couldn't afford an engine rowed their longboats, weighed down with rice or with scrap metal from the riverbed, peddling seemingly effortlessly at oars that must have been at least fifteen feet long.

Sampans pulling pontoons laden with sand, the military naval grey of the rusting gunboats, the high cranes, the ships that anchored in the fair lane and the twin spires of Saigon's French legacy, a Roman Catholic cathedral, along with the faded colonial houses with balconies, ornate entrance halls and courtyards, the romantic doorways with elaborate mouldings – created a unique atmosphere, an atmosphere sharply contrasted in the city itself, which has no high-rise buildings and still the vestiges of painted soft ochre, orange, and *bleu de ciel* of French colonial architecture. The strong original primary colours are now muted, to faded blues, pinks and burnt siennas.

Stepping from the silence of my room into the street and into the heat was like walking into a wall of warm marshmallow. The streets were teeming with mopeds, bicycles and three-wheeled, passenger-carrying cyclos. There were few cars and most commercial traffic was US army trucks, industriously patched and mended.

Telephone wires and power cables drooped from porcelain bobbins like dirty, twisted spaghetti. There were few advertisement hoardings. And the pavements were alive with street vendors selling soups and noodles from charcoal braziers with sizzling pans. There were cyclos waiting to have their punctured inner tubes vulcanised so that they could get back on the road in an attempt, often futile, to earn a dollar a day. They vulcanised the tubes using a press heated over charcoal.

I climbed into my air-conditioned Mercedes Benz. I was going to a highly esteemed restaurant. As the car pulled out into the jammed wide street, at this rush-hour time, the multitude of motorbikes, bicycles, cyclos and three-wheeled scooters turned into trucks with fourteen people clinging on, parted and scattered like a shoal of dace or roach being pursued by a marauding pike.

We swerved past a 'road up' sign where a gang of diminutive women dressed in loose blue overalls and the ubiquitous straw hats were cold-Tarmacking the surface by hand. They were tapping it in place with flat wooden pestles.

With much hooting and swerving, cursing and speeding, we finally reached the restaurant. The waiters, in neat black trousers, black shoes and white cotton shirts and ties were resting, lolling or snoozing around the tables in the courtyard. As our car crunched through the gravel-strewn pathway, they leapt into action, instantly alert, instantly attentive.

The manageress was there to greet me and invited me to the kitchen. In a covered yard behind the kitchen, instead of what you would expect to find in a European restaurant – that is to say, refrigerators and deep-freezes – here there were just cages.

Paul (the cameraman) and Steve (lighting) started setting up in the kitchen while the waiters, who kept a fascinated eye on their activities, began to dress the tables for the anticipated early evening rush of diners.

The dining room of the restaurant was a large, airy room with Formica-topped, steel-tubed tables covered in white cloths. On each table was a Bakelite ashtray, an aluminium paper serviette dispenser, a plastic tub of toothpicks and a bottle of soy sauce. In the centre of one wall was a red Formica dispense bar haphazardly covered with bottles of booze. Standing out among the bric-a-brac pertinent to such a bar – tumblers, ashtrays, little tin cup-size coffee filters (a hangover from the French occupation but still much esteemed by the Vietnamese whose mocha coffee, by the by, is among the best I have tasted anywhere in the world) – sat a small Buddha shrine with burning joss sticks. On the shelves behind the bar, between bottles of rice vinegar, fish sauce and neatly stacked piles of American cigarettes, there were over twenty glittering cheap Christmas cards, the style of Woolworths circa 1950.

In stark contrast to the dining room with its softly swishing ceiling fans, the kitchen was a dark, windowless lean-to shack. There were once tiles on the floor but most of them were now cracked and crumbled and had been replaced over the years by patches of concrete. The floor was black, slightly slimy, slippery and running in water. Half-a-dozen clay buckets were set on a rectangular step six inches off the ground. In these buckets charcoal was burning, filling the shack with a peat-like odour.

Cheerful, smiling women with bright clothes fanned the charcoal stones into life, their crow-like fingers clutching little woven fans. Boys and young men, in ragged jeans, flip-flops and dirty T-shirts bearing the legend Miss Saigon, were kneeling on the floor chopping vegetables and meat on concave, blackened, round chopping boards, simple discs cut straight from the trunk of a tree, with razor-sharp choppers called *dao thai*. Such washing-up as there was took place in a big plastic dustbin, erratically watered from a single brass cold water tap fixed by one screw to the wall.

There was a wonderful smell of ginger, garlic and lemon grass, chillies and coriander. I watched with a fascination that half made my taste buds run riot with delight and half gave me an overwhelming desire to throw up.

My hostess took me to look at the cages. To Western eyes – or certainly to mine, as someone, I might add, who is happy (well not happy, but feels no compunction in) killing, plucking and drawing a chicken, killing a lobster or boiling a crab – the cages were sickening. In one a python some twelve feet long lay coiled and motionless. In another a nest of small vipers squirmed. There was a cage of assorted rodents, but I couldn't identify them because I didn't have my *Observer's Book* of Vietnamese small furry animals with me.

The kitchen boy proudly ran a stick along the mesh of the cobra cage, hissing and goading them into a rage. They reared, heads darting, savagely attacking the wire that held them captive. The boy laughed. In what looked like a slatted wooden crate on a board feeding table, hung thirty or forty soft brown bats. By squatting on your haunches you could peer up at their baleful yellow eyes.

Overseeing this ghastly gastronomic menagerie, high on a perch sat a tethered monkey, happily hopping to the extent of his six-inch chain.

I say happily because in comparison to the others his lot was a good one – only the monkey was not for eating.

Dexterously, proudly, arrogantly, the young boy hooked a cobra from the cage and held it, with a broad smile to me. The cobra was hissing and angry, its tongue flashing rapidly. The teeth had not been removed.

My hostess was beaming happily. 'You like?' she said.

The crew were watching intently to see my response. They knew I was lying when I said, 'Yes, very happy.'

They took the cobra into the dark kitchen – it was now in even greater gloom since Steve had rigged a powerful light, which shone like a lighthouse on a murky night, to one of the charcoal stoves, upon which sat a wok filled with boiling water.

With a swift blow from his chopper, the boy took off the snake's head. I turned away at that point, but I think he slit the stomach and a few moments later I was proudly shown a glass of cobra blood. And in a smaller glass, the still pulsating liver or heart of the reptile.

The snake was quickly thrown into the boiling water to blanch. And as soon as it had stopped writhing it was removed, scaled and deftly chopped into bite-size pieces. It was then thrown into a wok with oil, ginger, garlic, shallots, chillies, palm sugar, fresh nuts, crunchy vegetables and noodles. So swiftly that I couldn't catch what they were, the cook turfed in drops from unmarked bottles, which I think contained soy, fish, and possibly chilli sauce.

The dish was transported with great ceremony to the table and I, in my Graham Greene suit, my Jermyn Street shirt and silk bow tie, sat in desperate anticipation. I asked for a beer.

'No, no,' they said; 'you must drink the blood.'

The bottled remains of heart or whatever was also placed in a little shot glass on the table, in my honour. One stroke of luck occurred when a waiter, who wanted to show off his prowess, grabbed it from under my nose and swallowed it in one. 'It makes me strong,' he boasted. And he ran from the room.

But I was still frozen at the thought of a) having to eat the snake, b) drinking its blood. And also of losing face in front of these remarkable people. And delivering a meaningful piece to camera. In years now of making these programmes, it was without doubt the worst moment.

I appealed to David for help. 'You must do it, we have come this far, we can't go back,' he said.

The entire restaurant staff sat in a jibbering semi-circle behind the camera, waiting to see what would happen – when Steve, under the pretence of adjusting something under the table for some technical reason, grabbed the glass of blood as if he couldn't resist it, as if all his life he had wanted it and drank it in one. I feigned disappointment and chided him for depriving me of such a treat and managed, following his example, to eat a piece of snake, which tasted like frog's legs.

Feeling bad in the back of my limousine, the driver honking against the traffic, I remembered Peter Sellers' version of Rupert Brooke's poem 'The Old Vicarage, Grantchester': 'Stands the Church clock at 10 to 3 And is there cobra still for tea?'

SITTING IN A BAR, HAVING A JAR

It was good to get back into the air-conditioned sanctuary of the Saigon Floating Hotel. The hall porters, the bellboys and the security guards greeted us cheerfully. We took the lift to our room – or cabin – on the third deck, and nodded to the security guy who hovered by the ice machine in the passageway. He waved and, as we turned towards our room, I knew he ticked us off on his board.

James Spurway, an amiable Australian of about thirty, manager of the place, had kindly placed a bottle of Chivas Regal and a tub of ice on my sideboard. But first I drank a bottle of still mineral water to wash away the snake. And then in a hot foam bath I relaxed with a tumblerful of the amber liquid, listening to the cubes cracking. One of those wonderful moments of fantasy so often present on these trips. I was suddenly a Secret Agent, a spy, a Man with a Mission. I was on the point of making an important contact with some Vietnamese commanders, after weeks of coded messages, whispered meetings and shadowy figures in the dim backrooms of anonymous bars – when Shaunagh burst into the bathroom and said: 'You've been in there twenty minutes, is there any chance I can get washed too?'

Freshly bathed and changed, we went down to the noisy chromium bar where Australian gas engineers were bullshitting American oil ones while downing bottle after bottle of Tiger beer. Dotted around the bar, apparently chatting earnestly but surreptitiously checking out the foreign visitors, raven-haired Vietnamese women in black miniskirts and patent leather high-heeled shoes appraised the potential pickings.

It was that awful hour of the night, typical of south-east Asian hotels, when the Happy Hour cocktail pianist is mournfully singing Frank Sinatra or Nat King Cole, playing the electric piano, slightly off key, and the piped music from the empty coffee bar overlaps the valiant pianist's effort to create a cruel cacophony of sound.

People stared at us. There was a momentary pause in the conversation of the power-broking wheeler-dealers as Shaunagh walked towards the bar. She is tall, blonde and young, they were all fat and balding, the Aussies in shorts and Miss Saigon T-shirts, the Americans in tartan trousers and button-down collars with their ties pulled down. I knew they wondered who I was. Then I ordered a beer for Shaunagh and whisky for me – only two or three times before we got it right – from the helpful, smiling but uncomprehending Vietnamese bartender.

The pianist finished, someone turned off the music and there was just a murmur of conversation and the chink of glasses at the end of a hard-working day. But we were now sufficiently old-hand, at least as far as European-run hotels were concerned, to tell that any moment there would be a band, either Thai, Filipino or Chinese. And, sure enough, one came on. The girls, sexily dressed, and the boys in electric blue jackets, black bow ties, purple pants and white shoes, unemotionally – their eyes not smiling, their heads not moving – rendered faultless versions of the Beatles, Phil Collins, Tammy Wynette, John Denver and, of course, Abba. And, really, they were quite good.

Later, after we had been there a few days, I realised that I could set my watch by what tune they were playing. The highlight of my evening was at 9.15, after their break. By the way, it was only then that I realised how small they were because on stage, the girls in their high-heeled shoes and the boys in stack-heeled boots, they looked tall and elegant. But as they stepped into the bar to take a break they were dwarfed by the now garrulous businessmen.

But it was at 9.15 that I knew they would play, with renewed energy, my favourite song. It was an Abba song that I thoroughly enjoyed. I didn't know the words, but it was very sing-alongable. I said to my wife, 'It's "Chicken Tikka" again.' It was some weeks before she let me into the secret shared by fifty-two million people throughout the years, with the exception of me, that it was not called 'Chicken Tikka' but 'Chi Qui Tita'!

My visit to the snake restaurant had made it a hard day and from the dazzling choice of the European smorgasbord in the coffee shop, the fine Chinese restaurant in the hotel, street food ranging from noodle soups, delicate Vietnamese spring rolls (small finger-size rolls of rice paper filled with minced chicken, prawn, finely chopped carrot or beansprout, quickly deep-fried, wrapped in a crispy, crunchy lettuce leaf and dipped into a fish sauce), an exciting plate of Vietnamese fried rice (so much more subtle than the Chinese version) or one of the other five hundred different dishes you could buy from the street hawkers – I unashamedly ordered fish fingers and chips in the coffee shop.

LOVE ME, LOVE MY SNAKE

The next morning I had a delicious breakfast of thin egg noodles stir-fried with shallots, shrimps and chillies and washed down with a bowl of spicy chicken consommé – basically made from chicken carcasses slowly simmered in water flavoured with tamarind, lemon grass and chillies and strained, after which the chicken is shredded from the bones and popped back into the clear broth. We then set off with our guides, interpreters and the lady from the Ministry of Culture to a Vietnamese Army camp.

Along the dusty flat countryside, past paddy fields, past little huts made of elephant palm, past roadside stalls roasting duck and pork, past piles of rear axles – the flotsam of the former American military presence – past mountains of bald but saleable truck tyres, past fences draped in rice paper like so much linen hanging to dry. Every kilometre there was one of those small white and red-tipped lozenges indicating the distance, a road marking system unchanged since the French. Men huddled around ancient lathes, regrinding crankshafts on the pavement. There were Renault Dauphines, *fourgons* and *fourgonnettes*, gaily painted De Soto buses, Citroën light Fifteens and big Fifteens, some immaculately restored and repainted orange, red and black, others in their original, now faded greens, greys and blacks, still valiantly carrying fourteen passengers, eight baskets and three bicycles.

As Saigon slipped further behind us, gradually the traffic thinned out to the occasional bicycle or trishaw and the odd pedestrian. Through one village, which had a rare strip of macadam road, we passed a roadsweeper of perhaps forty years. He had no legs, instead he wore a leather cradle around his bottom. With one hand he hopped along the road and, holding a simple brush with the other, he swept leaves and cigarette ends in front of him. Soon we turned on to a rough red track and after bumping along for a hour, passing little thatched communes of a dozen simple huts and open stalls selling anything from bicycle tyres to noodles, we reached the army camp.

To my horror it was the Vietnamese Army's Medical Corps Snake Farm, where for humanitarian reasons they farmed poisonous snakes to extract serums for the thousands of Vietnamese agricultural workers who suffered serious snake bites while working in the paddy fields.

The idea was, according to David, that I would cook a Pork and Prawn Stew for the Vietnamese Army. It would be a coup, it would be a first, said he. So in about 120 degrees Fahrenheit, stripped to the waist, watched by a group of visiting politicians and generals, I set about preparing the dish. David had arranged for members of the volleyball team, practising for the military championships, to lob the ball on to the back of my head or into the pot, which they relentlessly did at various intervals. I also had my first glass of an extremely restorative drink that sends you completely gaga after two glasses, called cobra tonic.

But it was a fascinating dish and it revealed one secret of Vietnamese cooking that most cookery books fail to make clear. It is the question of cooking with sugar. The most important thing about the recipe is that you must caramelise the sugar in a little pot of oil so that it turns toffee-coloured, before you add the meat. This seals the meat, keeps in the marinade flavours it already has, and colours the resulting sauce. If you just let the sugar melt so it is a syrup you will not achieve the desired effect – so there, now read the recipe on page 162.

Opposite: **Top** Crab and Asparagus Soup (page 114); **Centre**
Prawn Soup – Spicy and Sour (page 110);
Bottom Meaty Cabbage Rolls in Soup (page 121)
Next page: Steamed Grouper with Chilli Sauce (page 131)

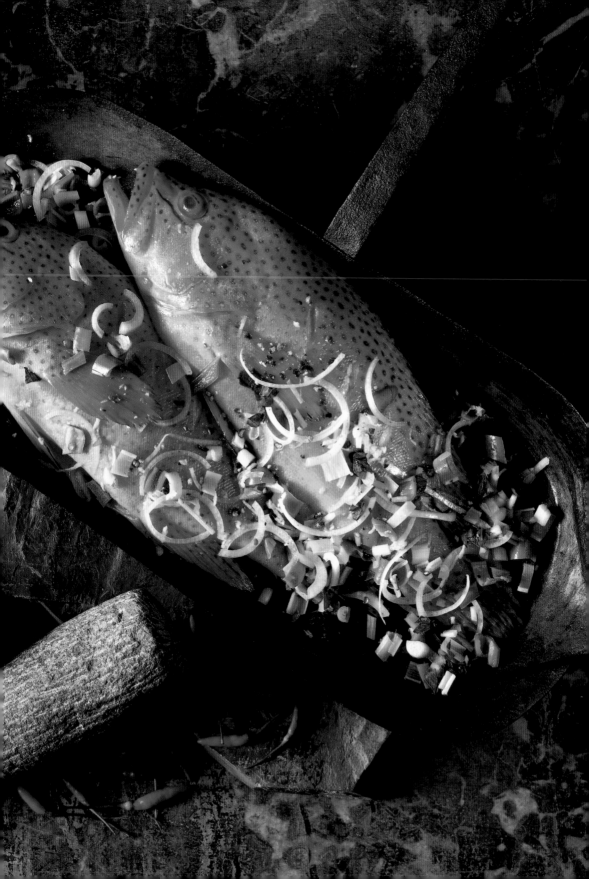

As a neat little epilogue, after the soldiers had downed their food and thoroughly enjoyed it, the General-in-Charge took me round his snake pits. It was one of those moments when, of course, I didn't have my camera, but it was a sight to see Shaunagh with a twenty-foot python around her. It was also quite something to watch a yellow and black ringed snake, whose bite can kill you in twenty minutes, being cuddled as if it was a newborn babe by the Vietnamese General. He explained, however, through the interpreter, that he had brought these snakes up from eggs and they loved each other like mother and daughters.

In an unguarded moment the General, who had taken a great liking to us, instructed the translator to tell us a little of his experiences in the War. And in an unguarded moment, she complied. To cut a long story short, in wartime the snakes formed a vital and deadly function of the Vietnamese military machine. Think about it.

It was then that I realised something about this happy smiling race, united now after a bloody war – wasn't it John Pilger who said most people think that Vietnam is not a country, but a war? – I realised that with their amazing energy, their savage ingenuity, ruthlessness in war but productivity and innovativeness in peace, there was no way that the Americans could ever have defeated them. I thought perhaps that Vietnam is the smiling snake – step on its tail and it will bite you, stroke it and it will love you.

Samui Oyster Fondue (page 148)

THE CYCLO

The best way to enjoy the colonial boulevards and avenues of Saigon, the only way to enjoy the crumbling French architecture, the only way to observe the street life without being pestered by twenty people at a time all trying to tell you something, is to put on your well-cut linen suit, a Panama hat, and hire a cyclo.

Cyclos are a Vietnamese institution; there must be thousands in Saigon alone. The cyclo is a three-wheeled bicycle. The driver sits conventionally, if somewhat uncomfortably, on a hard leather saddle over the rear wheel. But instead of using the regular handlebars of a bicycle, he steers by pushing the bar of the two-wheeled pram, which contains one seat. So you hop into the front of this thing like an impoverished potentate. A little fold-up canvas hood protects you from the sun or the rain. The machine has no gears, and the only braking system is a lever-operated rear drum brake. Some cyclos are beautifully painted or chrome-plated, others are old and rusting, with flaking pale blue paint.

There is an enormous rank of cyclos outside the Floating Hotel and as you walk up to select one, the riders swarm round you shouting, 'Me, me, me, me, me.' The rider lifts the cyclo up from the saddle to tilt the pram forward to the ground so you can climb in comfortably and then pulls it back. He climbs on to the back and from a standing position, with massive effort, gets the thing rolling. Then he sits back on the saddle and pedals rhythmically, not altering the pace, irrespective of the gradient (fortunately, most of Saigon looks pretty flat – from the passenger seat, that is).

A couple of seconds after leaving the Floating Hotel is the first big adventure, as the rider swoops along with hundreds of others into the mêlée of repainted US army trucks, lovingly restored US jeeps, bicycles and mopeds that forms an enormous roundabout. No cyclo rider looks at another, no hand signals are given, cars and lorries are ignored. It is absolutely hair-raising. And as I have said before, there is no lane discipline, you can come from left to right or right to left, there are no traffic lights, there is no Highway Code of any kind. And yet in all the rides I had in Saigon and all the miles I travelled there I didn't even observe a near miss, let alone any kind of accident.

For the first few minutes you feel a bit embarrassed, posing with a long cigarette, taking pictures of the architecture and the street life, pausing to buy a wonderful Vietnamese delicacy, such as minced prawn barbecued on a piece of sugar cane, which, by the way, is actually an extremely simple thing to do. You get a load of fresh shelled shrimps, chop or mince them finely (don't use a blender, it makes them too mushy). You add a bit of salt and pepper, a dash of fish sauce, bind the whole mixture together with some beaten egg white, squeeze it evenly over a piece of sugar cane about six inches long and barbecue it over a charcoal fire. And just munch as you go along. But this feeling of embarrassment is quite real, as I say, for the first few yards, because you are asking another human being to do the work of an animal. And even these days, if the rider worked all day, which would mean cycling many, many, many exhausting miles, he would be lucky to earn one US dollar.

We pedalled up a street that specialised in shops selling lacquer boxes, screens and friezes and allegedly authentic Zippo lighters with their ghoulish inscriptions, supposedly recovered from the bodies of dead GIs. Methinks that twenty years or more after the end of the War, these are the result of a Vietnamese entrepreneur who has realised how gullible the American tourists can be. And talking of being a tourist – I adore shopping in foreign places. So I stopped to buy some lacquer boxes.

Incidentally, on the subject of lacquerwork – whatever kind and the Vietnamese are extremely good at it whether it is little pin boxes, oblong boxes to put playing cards or knitting needles in, boxes just for decoration or lacquered vases – a word of advice. There is cheap lacquerwork and then there is good lacquerwork. And the way to distinguish one from the other is as follows. Take, for example, a rectangular box with a hinged lid, tip it upside down and look at the bottom of the box. If the lacquer runs smoothly and without interruption from the side of the box right across the bottom it is a cheap lacquer box. If, on the other hand, there is evidence of a faint seam running around the edges of the bottom so that the lacquer is very slightly stepped, you have a good-quality lacquer box. This is because, with the cheap ones, the lacquer is applied directly to the wood, albeit in several coats. Lacquerware that will last after the box has been made has been covered very carefully with a thin fabric and then lacquered. The fabric has the effect of binding the wood so that it can never distort.

If you stop for a coffee or to do a little shopping, your cyclo rider (or driver) will wait for you. Don't worry that you cannot remember what he looks like when you come back from the shop, because he will not forget you. You are, after all, a dollar – and all dollars look the same!

You can't easily spend any money in Saigon, you get thousands and thousands of dong for a dollar, and artifacts and gifts and such stuff are really cheap. But it is essential to haggle, even if, like me, you prefer not to and are happy just to say 'How much?', give the man the money, wrap it up and go. Buying and selling, for the Vietnamese, is as much of an art form as sculpture or music.

You don't need to know the names of any of the streets in the commercial areas, you just need to know them by what they sell. There is a street that just sells shoes, one just clothes, another just books and stationery, another just electrical goods. I bought a hand-made guitar for £8. I could have had it for £3 if I had haggled properly, but it works and it is fun.

We stopped for coffee at a pavement café. Strong mocha coffee, which is really good, with a freshly fried doughnut (or should I say *beignet*, yet another legacy of the French), light as a feather, warm and rolled in sugar. It was delicious. I also had a glass of local sugar cane rum. It was thick, sweet and hot and the colour of some amber jewel.

Thus fortified, we set off once again, at a steady pace, the cyclo creaking, to the Exhibition House of Aggression War Crimes. In the gardens of the museum is a collection of US tanks, helicopters, flame throwers, bombs, rocket launchers – the ghastly machines of war. Standing like statues, the ghastly tools of destruction. And for good measure, a blatant statement of anti-French sentiment, there is also a guillotine, which was in use right up to the 1960s. Stand by that quietly, half close your eyes, and A Tale of Two Cities will make you shudder.

The museum itself, with its photographs, exhibits and facts, is for those with strong stomachs. There is a plaque on the wall which says:

> In their aggression in North Vietnam the US imperialists have dropped 7,850,000 tonnes of bombs down to two parts of Vietnam, north and south. They have used all kinds of weapons such as GP bombs weighing 250 kilos, 500 kilos, 700 kilos, to the cluster and fragmentary bombs. They have also used weapons killing people by blasting force, by the burning of oxygen such as in the 1000" bombs, the CVU 55 B bombs. This is not to mention the various kinds of shells, the napalm bombs, the phosphorus bombs, the chemical toxicants, gases. The US shells and bombs have killed, wounded and disabled millions of Vietnamese, devastated hundreds of thousands of villages. US Professor Westing has estimated that south Vietnam has approximately 25 million bomb craters.

Needless to say, there is no reference to what the Vietnamese did to the Americans, no mention of camouflaged pits with razor-sharp bamboo sticks in them, no mention of snakemes and other devices. But under the circumstances it is pretty hard to criticise them for that. The Vietnamese will tell you that for over two thousand years they have been invaded repeatedly – repeatedly invaded, but never conquered. And until 1989 they were fighting with Cambodia and Laos.

I wonder, now that there is more and more evidence of a free market economy and increasing foreign investment, how long it will be before (if the Americans lift their sanctions and flood the place with much-needed money) the communist government will modify a few things.

LUNCH AT THE REX

Street food in Vietnam is exciting and inexpensive. Little dishes like ground beef wrapped in vine leaves and deep-fried, something like Greek *dolmades*. Or a prawn and lotus-shoot salad, tantalisingly flavoured with lime juice, fish sauce and chillies. Or the simplest of pancakes made from a batter of rice flour, saffron and water that when cooked in the hot fat looks like a yellow lace doily and is filled with stir-fried beansprouts, prawn and small cubes of pork fat. Or a bubbling steamboat of any variety of *pho*. All absolutely divine. You might get a chilled beer or more likely a warm beer with a great lump of ice stuck in it. In fact, it is quite common to have drinks served with ice in it even if it is not appropriate.

The downside of eating on the street is that they fire the dishes at you so fast that you have to eat up and go. There is no ceremony to eating at this level. It is quite saddening, but I suppose totally practical, that so much love and effort is put into the preparation of these dishes, which are eaten so quickly. Here you eat to live, not live to eat. Talking and other forms of recreation take place elsewhere.

So every now and again you tend to hanker for a proper restaurant where you can have an apéritif, smoke a cigarette and linger over a menu and talk. But there aren't many restaurants as we know them, and it is usually only in the hotels that you will find them. And, of course, most hotels don't cater for the local population but for foreign tourists and business people, and they modify their menus accordingly. The exception to this rule, however, is the elegant Rex Hotel, which is situated on the corner of Nguyen Hue and Le Loi, but could quite easily be on the Boulevard St Germain in Paris. It is a hotel of many facilities and restaurants, but the Vietnamese restaurant, with carved

Buddhas, parrot cages, carved teak friezes, tiled floor and hand-made Oriental china, is a splendid amalgam of French and Vietnamese decor. A veritable legend in its own lunch time!

The restaurant has an extensive menu which my Editor – as all editors who specialise in food – would absolutely adore, because it is divided into three: the cooking of North Vietnam, the cooking of South Vietnam and the cooking of Central Vietnam. And, dear Editor, do you know that the only thing all editors ever go on about is the regional variations of cuisines in any given country. What they fail to realise is that here in the twentieth century, because of things like aeroplanes, lorries, trains, refrigerators, regional cooking has gone out of the window! And you can just as easily eat duck Hanoi-style in Mandalay, Paris, Peking or London as you can in Saigon. Anyway, I digress.

For lunch in this cool, elegant dining room, we had a fascinating feast of such variety of flavours and textures, of such lightness and such tongue-tingling seasonings than I have tasted in a long time. So if you are sitting comfortably and, I hope, feeling hungry, maybe this will excite you too.

By the way, the opinion of gastronauts in concentric circles is that despite the many influences on Vietnamese cooking, it is essentially a skilful blend of Thai and Chinese cooking, with a massive slice of Vietnamese flair and individuality. And if I hadn't believed it before, I certainly was convinced after this lunch.

At the start, Shaunagh had something which sounds so simple, a shrimp and pork salad. It consisted of exquisitely fresh, inch-long peeled boiled shrimps, a few tablespoonfuls of minced roast pork, a handful of fresh lotus sprouts, some finely grated carrot, some shredded cucumber, a few chopped mint leaves, a finely chopped chilli, and a little finely sliced spring onion. All of this was tossed in a light

coconut vinegar and placed in what looked like a blue and white Ming bowl. A Thai version of such a dish would be very similar, except that the dressing would be made from chillies, fish sauce, lime juice and sugar, and it would be heated and poured over the salad at the last minute.

I, me, myself – I had salted prawns to start with. They were much larger prawns, about two inches long, which had been salted and then fried in caramelised oil so they were slightly brown and slightly crunchy from the caramelisation process and the salt and the sugar. And they were just sautéed with some finely chopped chillies and garlic. Compare this refined version of caramelised prawns with sautéed salted prawns in a Chinese restaurant, where they simply dip shell-on prawns in salt and fry them very quickly, and serve them with a soy sauce dip garnished with chillies on the side. So you are beginning to see, I hope, that the Vietnamese have toned down the excessively hot and spicy Thai salad to suit their own subtle tastes. They have taken the fundamental and rather ordinary Chinese prawn dish and lifted it into Heaven.

Before our main course we decided to have a *pho* to share between us. This one wasn't the noodle and beef variety, it was fresh crabmeat and vermicelli. The clear broth was fishy and tangy, quite light, allowing you to enjoy the sweet flavour of fresh crabmeat. The soup was garnished with coriander and mint. Again, it was a more delicate and more truthful version of the Chinese-style Mongolian hotpot into which, it is well known, the Chinese will put anything that walks, swims, flies or crawls – ho, ho! How many times have you seen on your Chinese restaurant menu twice-boiled chicken, twice-boiled shark's fin soup or twice-boiled chickens' feet? This is done with the sound intention of extracting the maximum flavour from the basic ingredients for the soup, but it is so much heavier and less subtle in comparison.

Now the unusual, for me at least, pork dish that I had as my main course, took one slice of Chinese cookery and one slice of Thai cookery and fourteen Vietnamese rosettes. (The Thai influence here is the coconut milk.) They had roasted some loin of pork that they had allowed to cool. When I ordered the dish the pork was simply boiled in coconut milk to reheat it. Thus I had a tender, succulent piece of pork, with a rich gravy of pork juices and coconut milk, lightly seasoned with salt and pepper. And this was served with pickled cabbage (a great Chinese preparation), crunchy pickled spring onions and steamed rice.

And I reckon that for Shaunagh's dish of grilled chicken and lime leaves they must have raided some Arab kitchens. Boneless, bite-sized pieces of chicken were placed individually on small, dark green lime leaves, and grilled. So what, I hear you cry. Well, before they placed the chicken on the lime leaves they marinated it with sugar, garlic, fish sauce and chopped chillies. After it had been grilled the chicken was slightly brown, the leaves singed at the edges and the marinade made a light, tasty sauce. Very probably there were both Arab and Thai influences in that dish (I think I will become a food historian!). And, of course, there was some slightly sticky, fragrant steamed rice.

Now, dear Reader, here's another thing the hungry foodwriter's editor craves for – it's a dessert. 'Give me lots of desserts,' she says, 'some exquisite confections prepared by a brigade of chefs in crisp white overalls.' But sad to tell, dear Editor, after meals like that in countries like this, they simply bring you a table about forty-eight feet long by six feet wide, piled to the ceiling with fresh fruit – some of which is still in its skins and some of which has been peeled and sculpted into shapes of elephants, Buddhas, or just squares and triangles. Then they bring you a fine coffee cup upon which sits a battered tin *cafetière* that drips thick mocha coffee into your cup.

THAILAND

The immigration hall of Bangkok airport was crowded with travellers from all over the world. There were backpackers wearing brightly coloured jackets and silk bandannas; Buddhist monks in their orange robes, with shaved heads; businessmen in lightweight suits, with light-weight suitcases; nuns, soldiers, sports teams uncomfortably wearing their new team blazers, sailors and diplomats (lucky bastards, going straight through a special channel while we shuffled slowly to the desk, shoving our bags with our feet); missionaries, priests and bishops; oil rig workers and construction engineers; women in sarongs, chieftains in robes, Arabs in fezzes – and the screech of multilingual conversation was shrill and discordant, as if a huge flock of starlings was attending an international conference.

We had been waiting in line for more than half an hour and had progressed only two or three feet when two men – one in a neat charcoal-grey suit, the other dressed as a security guard, complete with gun and walkie-talkie – marched briskly towards the desk. They made a comical sight; they weren't quite running but they were going at a rate of knots. They showed passes, spoke briefly to the immigration officer, rushed through the gate and came straight to Shaunagh and me.

'Welcome to Bangkok, Mr Floyd. Come with me. And Mrs Floyd too.'

I had no idea who they were, but they grabbed our luggage and barged their way to the front of the queue. We gave our passports to the armed guard and shot off with the other gentleman who, before we knew what had happened, was holding open the door of a choc-olate-brown Rolls Royce. We didn't know if we were being hijacked, arrested or kidnapped, it didn't seem to matter very much. Watee, as the man in the dark suit was called, turned out to be the assistant manager of the hotel we would be staying at.

'But what about our luggage and our passports?'

'No problem, leave it all to me,' he said smilingly, closing the door.

I hadn't noticed that the car had two other occupants in it, the driver and owner of the car, Khun Adul, and an English girl who introduced herself as Fiona Harris and proferred us two cut crystal glasses foaming with Krug champagne. Khun Adul was also one of the owners of the hotel. He was a pleasant, witty man and, as we set off into the choked traffic of the freeway into town, he made us feel welcome and enter-tained us with snippets of information about Thailand.

Finally, I plucked up the courage to ask Fiona who or what she is. It was a bit embarrassing when she explained because many months previously, apparently, I had met her at a travel exhibition in London, where she had introduced herself as being part of the Imperial hotel group in Thailand, and should I ever need any assistance if we were to film there, please give her a call. I am afraid her card, like most which are thrust into my hand on such occasions, was promptly filed in the bin. She had quite by chance followed up our meeting by calling my agent to offer the same proposition, and though I was not aware of it, she happened to call on the day it was decided that we would indeed be filming in Thailand.

The traffic police were stationed at almost every intersection of the motorway, their big shiny motorbikes gleaming in the sun. And they, with their large white crash helmets, anti-smog masks, tinted goggles, their perfectly tailored uniforms and cavalry boots, looked like inter-galactic storm troopers from Star Wars. But as efficient as they looked, there was little they could do to speed or relieve the agonising grind of this motorised juggernaut that was inching its way into the city.

It took over an hour and a half to cover the few miles from the airport to the hotel, but sipping champagne in the air-conditioned luxury of the Rolls Royce caused us no pain and the journey seemed to fly by. I remember noticing that many of the brightly painted trucks we passed had ornamental riveting along the bonnets and around the mudguards. And thinking how drab and dirty British lorries are by comparison.

We swept into the entrance of the Imperial Hotel. Security guards at the entrance snapped to attention and delivered sharp impeccable salutes that would have made Field Marshal Montgomery's day. On the steps of the hotel was a reception committee of eight stunningly attractive women, dressed in exquisitely tailored Western clothes. They would have made a good front cover for *Vogue*. As we were introduced formally to each one, they hung garlands of flowers around our necks, and brilliantly woven bracelets of heavy white flowers on our wrists.

Photographs were taken and the ladies escorted us into a comfortable sitting room where the ordinary management (male, and of much less importance than these women) team awaited us.

'Would you like more champagne?'

'No, I'd rather not,' I replied. 'I'd really enjoy a whisky.'

And in that moment was born a catchphrase and a tradition that stayed with us every day during our stay in Thailand and is now being used regularly in my own pub. My request was for a whisky with ice and water. To the Thai the best whisky is Johnny Walker Black Label and so it was translated to the barman as 'One big black on rock, please'. The welcoming drinks reception lasted for about two hours. Halfway through, the crew, who had had to endure an hour clearing customs with all of their gear and who very kindly had looked after my luggage too, straggled in, hot, sticky and tired from a cramped minibus journey. They too were draped in flowers.

'Big black on rock.'

With great ceremony and dignity, Khun Chompunute, resident director and wife of the group's chairman Khun Akorn, showed us to our room. To call it a room was, to say the least, an understatement. Apartment would have been more appropriate, the sort of apartment that you imagine people like Elizabeth Taylor have reserved for them in hotels around the world. Bedrooms, bathrooms, kitchens, another bottle of champagne. The place was heavily perfumed with exotic flowers. And in the corner of the sitting room was a well-stocked bar that would have shamed some of the pubs I know around me in Devon. I have never experienced such a warm welcome anywhere in my life before.

Fiona phoned to say that a table was reserved for us in each of the hotel's six restaurants – that is to say the European restaurant specialising in French food, the Japanese restaurant, the Chinese restaurant, the Thai restaurant, and the coffee shop/brasserie and the Shabu-Shabu restaurant, which I discovered later is an Asian steamboat place. They provide you with a steamboat bubbling with spicy stock and you select such ingredients as you would like to cook in it from fifteen or so stalls around the room. Beef, chicken, pork, fish, shellfish, vegetables, noodles, strange fruits, etc., etc.

We elected to eat in the Thai restaurant that night and get down to some serious research. But by the time we had unpacked, showered, changed and installed ourselves at the hotel bar, the tedious wait at Saigon airport, another boring flight and the drinks at the reception party, began to take their toll, and I was not really in the mood for serious eating. Egg and chips and a cup of hot cocoa and then heads under wings and wings under blankets would have been a more appropriate thing to do.

As I write this, some three months after the event, I can recall only one part of the meal we had that evening. But it was a dish of such stunningly contrasting sweet, hot and sour flavours that I will never forget it. In comparison to most people I lead a very privileged life. Good tables in the best restaurants throughout the world are easily available to me. I am afraid that I become quite blasé about food, so when I am genuinely gobsmacked by a new dish, it is a real treat.

Piled on the plate were assorted leaves – some sweet, crisp hearts of lettuce, others bitter like oak leaf and chicory, and others, like some variety of spinach, quite metallic – trembling with freshness. Scattered throughout were fine matchstick-size batons of spring onion, crunchy cucumber and celery. On top of that, garnished with celery leaves and chopped red chillies, were slivers of warm barbecued breast of duck. Over this was poured a warm dressing made from fish sauce, fresh lime juice, chillies, shallots and palm sugar (you will find the recipe on page 187). The hot and sour taste from the fish sauce and the chillies was explosive. And the tang of the lime juice sent shivers down my spine. After the first mouthful, I could not stop eating until I had demolished the entire dish. I didn't even pause to take a sip from my glass of iced Singha beer.

BANGKOK

The next couple of days were spent in traffic jams – sometimes in a minibus, sometimes in a Rolls Royce, sometimes in a chauffeur-driven Mercedes Benz and sometimes in a tuk-tuk. A tuk-tuk, in case you haven't been to Bangkok, is a three-wheeled vehicle based on a large motor scooter. Indeed, it has handlebars, and behind the driver's seat there are a couple of passenger seats under a gaily painted awning. They look such fun when you see them bombing around the place, but unfortunately the fringes of the awning block your view so you have to crane your neck to peer out and, of course, you are constantly attacked by the omnipresent choking smog fumes. Most motorcyclists and cyclists and indeed many pedestrians, wear smog masks. And although the crew would depart from the hotel in three separate vehicles at the same time, everyone would arrive at the destination up to an hour apart.

We did all the things we had to do, all the pick-up shots of palaces and temples, market scenes and general views. And a couple of cooking sketches – under the critical but helpful eye of my chum Chom.

Khun Piengchom is a former chef to the royal household and now executive chef to the Imperial group, charged with the responsibility of maintaining high standards in their thirty or forty restaurants. She is a sophisticated but gentle lady with an encyclopedic knowledge of food and of Thai food in particular. If she had not taken me under her wing, I would probably have left Thailand as ignorant as I had arrived. And everything I now know about Thai cooking I owe to my chum Chom.

Some Notes on Thai Cooking

■ The Thais like their food very hot and ten different varieties of the world's hottest chilli peppers are grown in Thailand. But it was Portuguese traders who first introduced the chilli into the country.

■ Although the Thais have adopted the wok and the stir-frying techniques from the Chinese, Thai stir-fries are lighter, more spicy and are not thickened, as the Chinese ones are, with cornflour.

■ Similarly, there is a great Indian influence on Thai cooking. But whereas the Indians make their curry pastes from dried herbs and spices, the Thais pound fresh herbs and spices – for example, chillies, lemon grass, coriander root, lime leaves, ginger, garlic and shallots. The two preferred curry pastes are green and red. This is achieved by using predominantly green or red chillies!

■ For sweetening, palm sugar is used. And the sour fish sauce is invariably used instead of salt.

■ Curries are explosive and creamy. This is achieved by the generous use of coconut milk and coconut cream, instead of dairy products. Ingredients such as pork, chicken, beef or fish used in the curries are cut into thin slivers (Chinese influence), unlike the Indian style of cutting meat into chunks.

■ The clear Thai soups are fiercely hot and flavoured with a mouth-tingling mixture of lime juice, lime leaves, tamarind juice and fish sauce.

By now I had become used to working with Paul. I didn't see him much out of working hours because our Paul was a bit of a nightbird and he liked to frequent noisy 'establishments' on the dark side of town. But at work he was impressively calm and patient and took a great deal of trouble to make my life as a presenter as easy as possible. He was also pleasingly decisive. Consequently, I had the impression that we were working rather quicker and more efficiently than before. Having said that, it still seemed really, really strange, not having Clive on the shoot.

So far the crew had had no rows. I think this was largely Kora's influence, who not only looked after David as a royal nanny would look after Prince William, but was also a first-class communicator, rapidly distributing schedules, commands and countermands to us all.

Now that Tim's wife Sheila (who helped me on the American series) has presented him with a son, he has become even more pompous than he was before. Previously David spent a lot of time, and often me as well, sending Tim up in a variety of ways. But now, as he says, 'I am a father, if I want to lecture you two or tell either one of you off because you are behaving badly or being too argumentative, I shall do so.'

'Yes, Tim,' we say.

He and Paul have worked together before, which is a great asset.

And, of course, Steve, the embodiment of the corporate conscience, peace-keeper and pourer of oil on troubled waters, continues to be infuriatingly saint-like! He has an appalling cough and is definitely unwell, but he still does the work of three men.

Kora too is almost perfect, except for one unforgivable trait. It's not easy for me to tell you this, I'm ashamed and hurt to have to tell you that She is – I'll have to rinse my mouth out after I say this – A Vegetarian. I can't even get any satisfaction from her having to put up with plates of boring salad every day because the blasted hotel staff are so kind, helpful and thoughtful that they've provided her with a multichoice special vegetarian menu for her entire stay!

David was going through one of his dieting periods. 'No, no, no, I shan't have any noodles and duck. No alcohol, I'll just have water. No sweet and sour pork, I'll just have a slice of melon.'

Two hours later he was sitting disconsolately on his own, eating a slice of melon, while we all tucked into a massive feast. 'Do you think I'm looking better?' he asked.

'Dieting for two hours doesn't make a great deal of difference, David.'

There was gloom in the camp. Rob Page phoned from England last night to tell David that the photography was disappointing and dark. This was meant to be kept from me, but, of course, I already knew, I was just waiting to see how long it would be before – and if – David told me. Certainly, they had been having huddled technical conversations among themselves all morning and Steve seemed to be longer setting up the lights than previously. After several tense hours the subject was finally brought into the open and David and Paul assured me that Rob had the wrong end of the stick and there was absolutely nothing to worry about. But it really had set us back on our heels for quite a while.

We rented a longtail boat to film the city from the river. These long narrow craft, with high, bird-like beaked prows, are powered by massive, marinised car engines that have a direct drive to a propeller through a propshaft about fifteen to eighteen feet long. And to steer the boat you have physically to drag the engine and its trailing prop, left or right. They go at a hell of a rate.

I was thoroughly enjoying myself being filmed hurtling up and down the river, but Paul waved me back to the shore and told me off for standing in the bows of the boat, like General Patton in his jeep leading his armoured division into battle. I said, 'I was playing Sanders of the River.'

But David said I had to play John Betjeman of the River, and sit thoughtfully in the middle of the boat.

Sometimes I think they are out to spoil my pleasure. But I tell you what, you can see more of Bangkok in ten minutes on a boat than you can in a two-hour car journey, which on a good day might get you two miles.

Outside the royal palaces and temples, Bangkok's architecture is drab 1950s grey concrete, apartment blocks and boring office buildings. The traffic is insupportable, the humidity and the smog is unbearable. But in direct contrast to that old cliché about France 'lovely country, shame about the people', Bangkok is blessed with as charming, friendly and hospitable citizenry as you could hope to find on God's earth.

Shaunagh, Fiona and I spent a few minutes playing millionaires, under the careful guidance of Khun Adul, in Bangkok's leading bespoke tailors. Even at these dignified and rarified heights, where you can spend hours feeling bolts of fine silk or pure English wool, it is necessary to haggle and barter. Indeed, if you don't barter at any level of shopping in Thailand, as throughout the East, the sales assistant or shopkeepers are genuinely disappointed. It is part of the way of doing things here. On the downside of shopping, the blasted wide-angle lens hood for my camera that I had been trying to buy since we left England, was also unavailable in Bangkok – but it was only a very small point really.

We made the obligatory visit to Patpong, Bangkok's red-light area. And though I am all in favour of big boobs and a bit of naughtiness we all agreed – even the unattached members of the crew – that it really was beyond the pale. And we went home early.

We visited what, according to the *Guinness Book of Records*, is the largest restaurant in the world. I think it seats four thousand people. It is Chinese and the waiters travel by roller skates. Every hundred yards or so there is a little stage, with bored young women enacting Chinese folk dances. Next time you are in Bangkok passing this establishment, my advice is that you keep going.

A very exciting place we visited, good fun for a gang of you to go to, is called the Fish Supermarket. As you enter you collect a trolley, as you would in any supermarket, and load it with everything that you would like to eat. At the checkout an assistant wheels it away to the open kitchen and gives it to one of the twenty or thirty chefs who then cooks it for you – and the joke is you pay for your meal twice, once for the ingredients and once for having it cooked. Khun Adul, who accompanied us almost everywhere, is the most easy-going fellow you could wish to meet, but he became furious when the Chinese proprietor refused me permission to cook in his kitchen. That was the only slightly inhospitable thing that happened to us in Bangkok.

The next day we were flying to north-west Thailand, virtually to the Burmese border, where they say the air is like champagne.

MAE HONG SON

On the plane from Bangkok to Mae Hong Son I was unfortunately recognised by an English passenger, who was determined to engage me in conversation about food. But there are times when I don't want to talk about it. So I managed to force him to talk to me about his job. He turned out to be an anthropologist. He was travelling to the Mae Hong Son region to continue studying one of the many hill tribes that live up in the mountains, close to the Burmese border, where in many cases the cash crop is opium. It was a fascinating hour. He told me that Thailand supported over one thousand varieties of orchids and that in 1991 Thailand exported nearly ninety million dollars worth.

The plane flew low over a mountain and my companion pointed through the window to a temple on the mountainside and said, 'It's a *wat*, which is a cross between a temple, a monastery and community centre.' Unfortunately, as he was enthusiastically describing the layout of a typical *wat*, I must have nodded off.

By the time I came round he was on to Buddhism and chattering about what is, apparently, the basis of the religion as preached by the Buddha in a deer park in Sarnath – to wit, or shall I say to wat – the four truths: one, the noble truth accepts that we shall suffer; two, the noble truth that there is a jolly good reason why we suffer; three, the noble truth that states this agony can be terminated as long as you accept the fourth noble truth, that it is essential to follow the noble eight-fold plan. In other words, take care how you speak, how you gain your living, and how pure your actions, efforts, mindfulness, concentration, opinion and intention are. Also important is the belief in karma and nirvana. And, of course, the code of non-violence, tolerance and compassion towards others is essential.

When I asked the Imperial group's chairman, Khun Akorn, how they have the courage or the nerve to develop their business so rapidly, he said, 'The trouble with you Christians is that you only do this life once, we Buddhists come back again and again and have plenty of time to put things right.'

This chap Anthony, for that was my fellow traveller's name, was good news. No sooner had we dealt with Buddhism, he was on to Siamese twins!

'Did you know', he said, 'the original Siamese twins, Eng and Chang, were born in 1811? And they were linked together at the hip. And they travelled the world as a freak show performing, among others, for Queen Victoria. They married South American twins and somehow managed to have, between them, twenty-one children. They became very, very rich and famous. Eng remained calm but Chang became an alcoholic and they were for ever arguing and fighting and even threatening to kill each other. They died from pneumonia in 1874.'

The descent into Mae Hong Son airport, through thick wooded mountains, their peaks obscured by mists, was terrifying. The plane dived and took tortuous steep bends and it was only at the last minute that the airstrip appeared in the valley.

Mae Hong Son is a sleepy little town, neat and clean, built around the intersection of two main roads. In this region there are very few indigenous Thai people; most of the population is made up of hill tribes who have over the years drifted from China and Burma. After the stifling atmosphere of Bangkok, the clean, fresh air here was a tonic. There are few people and even fewer cars. And the pine-clad mountains and the clear skies reminded me of Switzerland.

My chum Chom, with several of her colleagues including the irrepressible chef Somchai, was already at the hotel to greet us with garlands, champagne for Shaunagh and for me a bottle of Johnny Walker Black Label, a jar of ice, a glass and a bottle of still mineral water on a tray borne by a smiling waiter. He approached me, snapped his heels together, and presented the tray with the now immortal words, 'Big black on rock for Mr Floy.'

Pritchard was wearing a loose-fitting black silk jacket, black trousers, black shoes and an open-necked black shirt, his highly tanned face hiding behind a huge pair of sunglasses. Covered in garlands and sitting in a carved teak armchair, sipping champagne, he looked exactly like the nine-foot-high, carved Buddha that dominated the hotel foyer.

It was the King's birthday. The streets were decked with flags, the waitresses and waiters were dressed in their silk and multicoloured cotton finery. The red, white and blue national flags were pristine, the corrugated roofs were clean, the pick-up trucks were washed, the sun was shining and the palms were etched perfectly against the pale blue sky. The residents of Mae Hong Son were in their Sunday best. It was the most beautiful day. It was the middle of winter, and 85 degrees Fahrenheit. A big plane was flying over the thick electric cables that ran up and down the street.

To celebrate the King's birthday (a day on which no alcohol is served, so drinks come in teapots) we were having lunch in the Fern Restaurant in the main street of Mae Hong Son. It had a simple, clean, airy dining room with solid Formica-topped tables and green plastic chairs on black steel frames.

I had a mind-blowingly hot, creamy yellow curry of slivers of fresh bamboo shoot and chicken. Shaunagh had a green curry of chicken that was prepared with miniature aubergines, twigs of fresh peppercorns, lime leaves and green chillies, topped with a pinch of chopped fresh basil. We had another searingly hot salad with warm minced pork and a lime, chilli and garlic dressing. The waiters, watching us to see how we would cope with the spiciness of the food, virtually applauded when we wiped our plates clean and asked for more. Shaunagh, in particular, was developing a remarkable taste for hot food, often calling for an extra side order of chilli dip. At every meal we had in Thailand, we washed it down with what I think is one of the best bottled beers in the world, Singha beer. It comes in lovely cold brown litre bottles.

We stopped for coffee at a hotel, which was decorated with gaily painted carved Thai artefacts – carved musicians, carved fish, carved Buddhas. They weren't intended for sale, but Shaunagh persuaded them to sell us ten splendidly carved musicians, each playing a traditional Thai instrument. This impromptu shopping expedition took nearly three hours to negotiate. After the brilliant lunch at Fern's, we managed to acquire the art of bargaining – or maybe the Singha beers had something to do with it! I hope the King enjoyed his birthday as much as we did.

PS If you happen to be keen on Thai carvings, the best place of all to visit is Chiang Mai, the largest town in northern Thailand, where most of them originate – and are much cheaper than in Bangkok too.

HILL COUNTRY

At this time of year, December, the mornings are very cold and misty. And we were a grumpy, albeit silent, film crew that assembled in reception as dawn was breaking. The vans were loaded: one full of food, portable stoves and charcoal burners, under the control of Somchai, dressed for the occasion like a Thai royal bandit, complete with orange silk bandanna; the crew van, another Toyota truck; the equipment van: my toy jeep – one of those little Suzukis much favoured by hairdressers; a massive Shogun four-wheel drive jeep for my chum Chom; and a blue and white saloon for our armed police escort. We were going into the hills, virtually on the Burmese border, where it is considered dangerous to travel without police protection.

For the first two hours, we trundled along empty but made-up roads in the thick, dark mist. We overtook a convoy of ox carts dragging sacks of what I took to be rice going to some central depot. As the sun began to burn off the mist, we reached the foothills, which were planted with tea. A handful of men and women were scattered among the rows, picking leaves and depositing them in baskets slung across their chests. Our little convoy ground to a halt. It was obvious that David couldn't pass such a wonderful sight without stopping to film it. The only trouble was, the pickers were on the shady side of the road and David wanted them on the sunny side. Finally, after an hour of total confusion and misunderstanding, the pickers were persuaded to give up their legitimate labours and pose as tea-pickers in the sun, so they could be filmed more attractively.

The going was getting steeper now and the clay road was wet and slippery, like greased snakeskin. There appeared to be many new roads being built, gouged out of the mountainside. It was explained to me, somewhat irreverently, that since logging was now illegal, a neat ploy for permission to cut down the teak trees was to decide that some remote village required a road.

About noon, we reached a small dusty town called Soppong where, by some miracle, the two suckling pigs I needed for my cooking sketch later in the day were waiting for us. It was here that we also rendez-vous'd with the guide who was to lead us to the Lisu hill tribe village. He spent a few moments explaining that we must turn our vehicles about-face, drive two hundred yards and turn left into a track. But David, our leader, was playing with his new catapult and failed to pay attention to the instructions. Suddenly bored, he adopted his 'Wagon Train' persona, shouted the Pritchard equivalent of 'Wagons, ho!, follow me', leapt into his minibus and shot off.

We drove the two hundred yards to the turn-off point as the police car – sirens wailing, flags flashing, horns honking – overtook us at speed to try and recover David and the rest of the crew, who had disappeared into the distance miles ahead. He was finally retrieved and we set off on the twisting track to the mountains proper.

Although there is great pressure on the hill tribes to grow rice and vegetables – on our way up we certainly passed precipitous slopes cultivated with green beans and carrots on what looked to me to be very rich and fertile soil – their main source of income is derived from opium. This, when planted high up in the inaccessible hills between rows of carrots, is very hard to discover. It is for this reason that they live in such remote areas, to keep the law and authority at arm's length.

The higher we climbed the more dangerous became the track, with sheer drops of hundreds of feet to our right, makeshift bridges of roughly-squared rocks traversing deep gullies. Our hearts were in our mouths and our bodies were aching with the jolting and pounding of the vehicles over the pitted track. At last, we achieved a plateau and, following a barely discernible track, turned into a forest. It was the sort of forest where you would expect to see pythons sliding down trees and tarantulas crawling across the windscreen.

We drove for over an hour through the forest, and then started to climb again. The track stopped and gave way to a firm earth road with woven bamboo fences either side. Behind the fences were rows of beans. The road widened into a mud square, charcoal-brown, around which thirty or forty palm-thatched wooden huts were built. A family of small black pigs snorted and grunted in the square and a few chickens clucked and scattered as our vehicles approached. The place was deserted, but smoke was coming from the huts.

Within a split second of our arrival our vehicles were surrounded by the two or three hundred inhabitants of this village – the women in long, bright blue tunics with red sleeves, black knee-length pants and leggings. The children in scarlets, golds, vermilions and yellows, their dark faces blocked out with white sandalwood paste. They chattered and smiled and pointed and waved. The men, in black tunics with silver buttons, with gaunt, severe but handsome faces and black hair, stood behind the noisy throng of women and children. The village has no running water and no electricity, no radio, no television, no mechanised transport. To all intents and purposes we had just stepped back three or four hundred years in time.

Somchai and his men went to work immediately and within seconds had laid out a groaning plank with lunch – noodles and curries. Out of the corner of my eye I saw the silver tray with its Black Label whisky gliding towards me.

'Mr Floy, big black on rock, please.'

I was formally introduced to the head man of the village and presented him with a bottle of Johnny Walker Black Label. In turn he invited us into his house to take tea, fragrant green Thai tea. The water was boiled in a pot over an open fire that was set in the middle of an earth-floored, one-roomed hut. There was a wide wooden shelf a foot above the earth, which served as his bed. There was a small altar on the wall. His wife and another woman sat cross-legged beside the fire, pounding chillies in stone pestle and mortars. The room was smokey and purple wisps eventually found freedom through a hole in the ceiling.

With his sharp cleaver Somchai set about making a rudimentary spit in the centre of the village square and prepared a fire, watched by about twenty or thirty bright-eyed, motionless, silent children. They were quite beautiful children, and I had to stop myself singing 'Getting to

Know You' (from a film not held in the highest of esteem in modern Thailand).

The pig weighed about twenty pounds and, under my chum Chom's instructions, I made a paste of black pepper, coriander root, turmeric and salt. And I wiped this liberally inside the pig. Then in a pestle and mortar I crushed and bruised a handful of garlic cloves, skins still on, half a root of ginger and half-a-dozen lemon grass stalks. I mixed this

with a couple of handfuls of basil leaves and stuffed the pig. Somchai gave me some bamboo twine and I stitched up the cavity so the stuffing would not escape. The final preparation was to rub the skin thoroughly with a mixture of lime juice and soy sauce before I impaled the unfortunate pig on a piece of sharp bamboo and set it over the glowing embers of the fire.

While that is cooking, dear Reader, and it takes just two or three hours before the skin is crackly, golden and blackened here and there, let us just sort out this problem that most Europeans have about cooking rice. After my travels, I think the best all-purpose rice to serve is simply boiled rice. But you should buy either Thai jasmine rice or Thai fragrant rice. I can buy them easily enough – in fact, I use them in the pub – in both Plymouth and Exeter down in deepest, darkest Devon, so I have no doubt you can find it countrywide.

So that's the rice itself taken care of. Next, I recommend you invest in an electric rice cooker, which you can buy from Asian stores. This is a simple affair the size of a pressure cooker, with a removable, graduated cooking pot. To whatever mark you fill the pot with rice, you simply fill it with water to the level of the next graduation, put on the lid, switch it on, and forget it. Because when the rice is cooked, the pot switches itself off and keeps the rice warm and in perfect condition for up to six hours.

But to make the rice even better, what you must do is thoroughly wash it in cold running water until the cloudy, milky-coloured liquid gives way to fresh, clean water again. Strain carefully and put it into your rice cooker. Then instead of using just water, dilute a can of coconut milk to the consistency of watery milk, pour it over the rice, add a pinch of salt and cook away.

When the machine clicks itself off from 'cook' to 'keep warm', comb through the rice with a fork to separate the grains. This, I can assure you, will give you a bowlful of rice that is authentically Eastern. And with the minimum of fuss.

The sun was beginning to set, bleeding orange like the monks' robes, across the darkening mountains. The pig was crisp and aromatic. Another fire – a big blazing festival fire – had been lit and the village people were sitting around it. Musicians began to play a haunting, lilting melody on drums, pipes and mandalin-type instruments. The pig was cut and distributed and the chief pronounced it 'good'. He commanded the musicians to play and the dancers to dance and, as dusk fell into black night, I sat by the fire as they danced and played in a circle around me.

Endpiece: The following day we learnt that while the village was celebrating with us, military helicopters attacked and destroyed their entire crop of opium, beans and carrots, which were a further five miles up in the hills. They evidently knew it was happening, but it didn't interfere with the day's celebrations in our honour. Perhaps that's Buddhism.

KO SAMUI

Until 1988 the palm tree fringed tropical desert island paradise of Ko Samui was a pretty well-kept secret shared by the locals and a few well-heeled New Age International Travellers. It is a spectacular island with wonderful beaches and bays, inhabited mainly by coconut farmers and fishermen. When the airport was built, Ko Samui opened its doors to the world. Hotels were swiftly built and a rapidly growing tourist industry began to overtake the island's traditional industries of coconuts and cashew nuts.

I suppose that those early prospecting hippies would say the place was now ruined, but it didn't strike me that way – thanks in part to the influence of my friend Khun Akorn, who persuaded the local authorities to insist that no building could be built higher than a coconut palm. So happily Ko Samui has been spared the fate of so many other beautiful locations – the dreaded high-rise hotel. Approach any part of the island from the sea and you are confronted with golden beaches and swaying palm trees.

Although the island is only approximately fifteen kilometres by fifteen kilometres, it exports two million coconuts a month. The coconuts are harvested, not by man or machine, but by highly-trained monkeys, which scamper up the palms and throw down the ripe coconuts. A Division One monkey can harvest up to one thousand a day. The coconut palms are so prolific I seriously thought of wearing a crash helmet during my stay. A coconut hitting you from sixty or seventy feet would not be a joke.

Apart from making coconut cream, such an essential part of Thai cookery, the other main commercial use of the coconut is to produce copra, which is used to extract oil for cosmetics, cooking and canning.

What happens to the rest of the tree is maybe best expressed by the well-known North Country saying, that as with the well-butchered pig, 'there is nowt left but the grunt'.

The timber from mature trees is used to build furniture, fences, houses etc. The hair on the husk is used to make ropes, the shells are used as planters or polished and crafted into jewellery (pendants, necklaces), cooking utensils, soup bowls – you name it. The coconut palm yields one final treasure, but not until it dies – that is the palm tree heart. It has a slightly nutty flavour and is crispy, a bit like fresh bamboo shoots. On Samui it is often sliced and stir-fried with chillies and garlic or served in creamy coconut soups.

The interior of the island is pretty barren and all the fun takes place in the ramshackle bars and villages along the coastal strip. Motorbikes are cheap to hire, as are four-wheel drive jeeps. Everybody on Ko Samui, residents or visitors alike, are appalling drivers. We had only been on the island for about two hours before David and Paul managed to crash their newly-acquired motorbike, resulting in David being extremely uncomfortable for some days. But bless his heart, he barely whimpered. Much.

We all had exquisite rooms overlooking the beach and the ocean. In fact, they weren't rooms, they were well-appointed, well-made cabins set among exotic shrubs, trees and flowers. Santana, the General Manager of the Imperial's three hotels on the island, greeted Shaunagh and me at the airport and announced he would be at our disposal throughout our stay. And my goodness, he was true to his word. We had our own air-conditioned minibus, plus chauffeur and Santana as guide. A bar was installed in the vehicle with gin, Black Label, beers, Cokes, mixers and ice. It was only when travelling that I was put to the inconvenience of having to pour my own drinks, because the moment we stopped at the location a smart waiter, in black trousers and white tunic, was waiting at the side of the vehicle with the silver tray and ubiquitous 'Large big black on rock'!

The weather was beautifully warm, not too humid, and each evening at supper-time there was a splendid, refreshing, offshore breeze. We were all tranquillised into a stupor by the happy feel of the island and none of us was in the frame of mind for any kind of work. After two months on the road, we were in the mood to party. Unfortunately, though these trips sound exciting, we are all paid to entertain the viewers; we are not paid to amuse ourselves. So we girded the corporate loin and set about cooking Beef and Cashew Nuts on a Desert Island, zooming around the archipelago in a high-speed motorboat and a luxury yacht!

We did a wicked anti-hippie sketch with me driving a large jeep dressed like the District Commissioner. As usual my chum Chom was there, showing us how to make Pineapple and Mussel curries served and eaten from the pineapple shell and other wonders. You will find the recipe on page 165.

We filmed a great sketch, making piña coladas with the help of a well-trained monkey. We got scratched and bitten on another island, foraging for herbs, wild fruits and vegetables. We corrupted our police escort with bottles of duty-free whisky. We filmed the temples and the Big Buddha, a massive golden creature sixty or seventy feet high, gazing over Big Buddha beach.

We were enchanted by the Thai staff of the hotel, rehearsing English Christmas carols for the imminent onslaught of December tourists. And I became a hippie for a day – dressed in bandanna, kaftan, waistcoat and beads, armlets and wristbands and little leather pouches.

On our last night we invited our helpers and friends from Malaysia – Awi and Hafiz and, of course, our friends from the island, and had a huge party. This was also the night that Fiona Harris, who had been so helpful throughout the entire trip, slipped a disc and was unable to join in the festivities. We filmed David cooking the farewell supper. We all got very drunk and emotional, vowed to become Buddhists and to come back to Thailand and the East, again and again and again . . .

Opposite: Sautéed Fillet of Sole with Green Vegetables in
Black Bean Sauce (page 126)
Next page: **Left** Lobster in Preserved Black Bean Sauce (page 142);
Right Fried Mussels (page 138)
Opposite page 97: Fried Fish and Ginger (page 132)

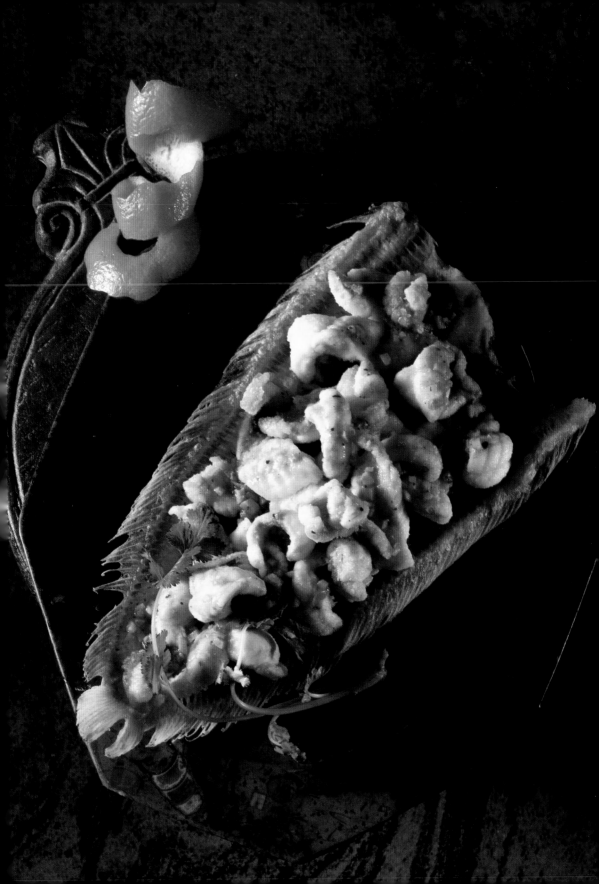

A NOTE
ON INGREDIENTS

AUBERGINE, BABY GREEN AND PEA Unlike the type usually available here, baby green aubergines are about 2.5cm (1 inch) in diameter, while pea aubergines are the size of marbles or peas. They are often green but may also be white, purple or yellow and can be found in some Oriental or specialist stores. If you can't find them, use ordinary large purple or yellow aubergines and cut them to the size of green aubergines.

BANANA LEAVES These large leaves can be obtained in Oriental stores. They are used for wrapping food and are sometimes made into containers for steaming. They give a delicate flavour to the food but are inedible.

BASIL, HOLY Holy basil, also called Thai basil, can be bought in Oriental stores. Thai 'holy' basil has darker leaves and a deeper, sharper flavour than the ordinary 'sweet' basil generally used in European cooking. If you cannot find holy basil, sweet basil may easily be substituted. Sprigs of fresh basil may successfully be frozen whole in plastic bags.

BEANCURD Often called by its Japanese name tofu, this is made from puréed and pressed soy beans and has a texture like soft cheese, but a bland flavour. It is, though, extremely useful in absorbing the flavour of other ingredients. Beancurd is normally sold in small, firm blocks in its liquid, which is discarded before using. There is a soft junket variety that is best used in soups. Solid beancurd for stir-frying should be carefully cut into cubes or shreds with a sharp knife. Too much stirring can cause it to disintegrate. Look for it in Oriental shops, health food stores and some supermarkets.

BEAN SAUCE Known as yellow bean and brown or black bean sauce as well, bean sauce is made from crushed yellow soy beans, mixed to a paste with flour, vinegar, spices and salt. It tastes quite salty, but has a spicy, aromatic flavour. Sold in jars and cans and available in large supermarkets under popular brand names – look in the Oriental foods section.

CHILLI PASTE These roast ground chillies mixed with oil and sold in small jars can be bought in Oriental or Thai specialist shops. They come in varying makes and colours and are often labelled 'Ground Chillies in Oil'.

CHILLI PEPPERS Fresh chilli peppers come in a variety of colours, from yellow to purplish-black, as well as different degrees of hotness. The flavour of their flesh mellows when cooked, but if you've added too many, there is, I'm afraid, little you can do to rescue a dish.

The general rule is the smaller the chilli, the hotter it is. Some of the world's hottest chillies are grown in Thailand including the tiny bird's-eye or dynamite chilli, which is just 1cm (½ inch) long. The seeds and ribs are the hottest bits so these are often discarded. But the heat and flavour of all chillies vary enormously, so it is a good idea to taste some to see and adjust the amount you're using accordingly. The smallest chillies are usually found in specialist stores whereas supermarkets tend to stock the larger, milder types. Do not do what I have often done, rub your eye while chopping one up. So remember, wash your hands!

When a recipe calls for dried chillies, you should either leave them whole or cut them in half lengthways and leave the seeds in. Dried chillies add quite a bit of oomph to a dish. Take them out before serving if you don't like too hot a flavour. They can be bought from supermarkets and specialist stores and they keep well.

Coconut The kind most usually sold here are the mature, ripe ones with their hard brown fibrous shells and milky liquid, though young coconuts can sometimes be bought in their softish, green husks, which makes them look like melons. The flesh of an immature coconut is much softer and more jelly-like and the liquid, called coconut water, clearer; coconut milk is something quite different (see below). The mature, brown-shelled coconuts are fine to use for the recipes in this book.

Freshly grated coconut gives vastly better flavour and texture than the dessicated kind. To use a fresh coconut, pierce one of the 'eyes' at the base of the coconut with a skewer or screwdriver and drain off the water. Tap the coconut sharply in the middle with a hammer or similar until it splits. Break it up into smaller pieces. Then, with a sharp knife, prise away the white flesh. Warming the coconut in the oven for 5–10 minutes can make this easier. Peel away the brown skin and grate or slice according to your needs. Grated coconut and coconut chunks freeze well.

Coconut Milk Coconut milk is one of the most important ingredients in Thai cooking, featuring in all types of dishes. You can buy coconut milk in cans from Oriental stores and this is by far the easiest to use. Make sure it is unsweetened. Otherwise, coconut milk is made by soaking the flesh of fresh coconut in boiling water or milk, then extracting the liquid. It is also possible to use creamed coconut (see next page), or dried, unsweetened (dessicated) coconut available from health food shops. Use ordinary silver-top milk to make the coconut milk rather than water – it will produce a much richer, creamier result. It will also produce the heavier coconut cream that will rise to the surface and can be skimmed off to use in various recipes.

To make about 250ml (9fl oz) coconut milk, heat 500ml (16fl oz) milk until almost boiling. Remove from the heat and stir in 225g (8oz) grated fresh coconut or unsweetened dessicated coconut. Allow to cool to room temperature, stirring from time to time. Pour through a sieve, using the back of a spoon to extract as much liquid as possible. If you need coconut cream, allow to stand so that this rises to the surface, then skim.

You can also use the leftover coconut again for further extractions, but these really will be thinner and less flavoursome. Treat coconut milk as you would fresh milk – keep in the refrigerator and use within a couple of days.

CREAMED COCONUT You can also easily buy blocks of creamed coconut, which are more concentrated than coconut milk. To make coconut milk from it, chop or grate, say, 75g (3oz) and then heat gently with 175ml (6fl oz) water stirring frequently until dissolved.

CORIANDER, LEAVES AND ROOT Did you know that coriander is the world's most popular herb? It is widely used in cooking all over south-east Asia, China, Japan, India, the Middle East etc. The leaves should be strewn over a dish just before serving or stirred in towards the end of cooking so their fresh, distinctive flavour is not lost. Although coriander is sometimes called Chinese or Thai parsley, English parsley is a very poor substitute for it. And many supermarkets as well as Oriental stores do stock coriander nowadays. Look for deep-green and not tired or wilting leaves. The leaves are best bought in large bunches rather than small packets and they will keep well if put in cold water in a cool place.

The roots have a more intense flavour than the leaves and are frequently used in Asian cooking, either finely chopped or pounded, in marinades, curry pastes and so on. They may be bought in Middle Eastern or specialist stores and usually come with leaves and stalks attached. The roots should be rinsed and dried and kept in an airtight container in the fridge where they will stay fresh for several days. If the roots are unavailable, substitute coriander stalks.

CURRY LEAVES These leaves are rather like bay leaves but thinner and not so leathery. They are olive green and very aromatic. They may be obtained, fresh or dried, all year round from Asian shops. They may be minced, torn or left whole, according to the recipe.

FISH PASTE This is a thick paste made from fermented fish or shrimps and salt, though many varieties are made and some have thinner consistencies than others. It is used in small amounts as a seasoning and is available from Oriental stores. You could use anchovy essence or paste as an alternative.

FISH SAUCE This is a fundamental flavouring for Vietnamese and Thai cooking and there isn't really a substitute. It is available in bottles from Chinese and Oriental stores. Fish sauce is salty and comes in several varieties such as anchovy, prawn and squid. The colour and flavour will vary slightly according to type.

GALANGAL In Thailand, galangal nearly replaces ginger as a spice. It is related to ginger but has a less pungent flavour. Galangal can be bought fresh from Oriental stores and needs to be peeled like ginger before slicing. It is also sold as a powder and dried – soak dried pieces before using and fish out and discard before serving. When substituting dried for fresh galangal in a recipe, use 1 dried slice or 1 teaspoon powder for each 1cm (½ inch) fresh specified in the recipe. You could also substitute with half the amount of fresh root ginger, which will give a more pungent flavour.

GHEE A type of clarified butter with a strong, sweet and nutty flavour, ghee is, of course, used extensively in Indian cooking. You can buy it ready-made from Asian grocers. If you want to make it yourself, then melt, say, 100–225g (4–8oz) unsalted butter in a pan over a low heat. Skim off any froth or impurities, then cook it very gently for 30–45 minutes, until the sediment at the bottom of the pan has become golden-brown. (This means the butter has caramelised and produces the sweetish flavour.) Strain through a sieve well-lined with muslin, then store in the refrigerator.

GINGER, FRESH ROOT The wonderfully refreshing, pungent, citrus-like aroma and flavour – as well as hotness – that fresh root ginger adds to all kinds of meat dishes, fish, shellfish, marinades and so on is only just beginning to be appreciated in Western cooking. It will transform even a dish of plainly cooked vegetables and it is, of course, indispensable to many Asian cuisines.

The pale-brown, gnarled skin has to be peeled, like a potato, before it can be grated, chopped, sliced, whatever. Fresh root ginger will keep in the refrigerator for a couple of weeks, but make sure when you buy it that the skin is firm and isn't at all shrivelled-looking.

KAFFIR LIME LEAVES The glossy, dark green lime leaves give dishes a lovely lemony-lime flavour. You can find them, packed in plastic bags, in some specialist Oriental shops – and it is well worth the effort looking for them – otherwise you can usually find dried lime leaves. The fresh lime leaves keep well and can be frozen. If the recipe calls for the leaf to be cut into fine strips this is best done with scissors. If Kaffir lime leaves are not readily available, use 1 teaspoon finely grated lime peel for 1 lime leaf.

KAFFIR LIMES About the same size as ordinary limes, these are dark green with knobbly skins. The peel is often used for flavouring but that of an ordinary lime can be substituted. Kaffir limes are available from Oriental stores.

KATSUOBUSHI (dried bonito fish) These are air-dried blocks of bonito fish. They are thinly shaved or grated before use. Packaged bonito flakes can also be bought (*hana-katsuo* or *kezuri-katsuo*). Find them in Japanese or Oriental stores.

LEMON GRASS This looks a little like a hard-skinned, elongated spring onion, with fibrous, grey-green leaves. It adds an intense, but not sharp, lemon flavour and scent to cooking. You can buy it fairly easily from the greengrocer's sections in supermarkets and from specialist stores. When a recipe specifies chopped or sliced, then the bulky part is the bit to use. Trim the end and slice finely. One average blade or stalk should give about 2 tablespoons finely sliced lemon grass. Alternatively, the whole stalk can be bashed hard with a knife handle to release all the flavour and then added while cooking; don't forget to take it out before serving. Stalks will last for about 2–3 weeks in the refrigerator. You could use chopped lemon balm leaves or grated lemon zest instead, but you would not get an authentic flavour. Powdered lemon grass is also available; it is often called sereh powder.

NOODLES Many varieties of dried noodles can be bought in Chinese or Oriental stores. The basic types are as follows, though most are interchangable in recipes:
Rice noodles or sticks
Medium flat rice noodles
Very thin rice noodles (rice vermicelli)
Egg noodles, sometimes bought in 'nests'
Very thin transparent or 'cellophane' noodles (mung, wheat, pea starch or soy)
Dried noodles need to be soaked in cold water before using and then they cook very quickly. The dry weight doubles after soaking.

If you are able to buy fresh noodles from your local Chinese store, then the only thing you need to know is that they do not need soaking before use and they are cooked in the same way and for the same time as the soaked dried variety.

OYSTER SAUCE Dark brown in colour, this thick sauce is made from a concentrate of oysters cooked with soy sauce, wheat flour, cornflour and rice. It has a rich flavour that is not fishy, despite its name. Often part of recipes for Chinese cookery, it can also be used as a condiment.

PALM SUGAR A coarse, thick brown sugar made from various palms. Sold in round cakes, it has a strong, slightly bitter caramel taste. If unavailable, use dark soft brown sugar or equal quantities of demerara and granulated sugars.

PANDAN **LEAVES** These are the long, dark-green, sword-shaped leaves of the Screwpine tree. Malaysian cooks often use them rather like vanilla pods are used in the West – indeed vanilla pods can sometimes be substituted. They have a fragrant scent and flavour rice and puddings. The distilled essence of the flowers of the Screwpine tree is called kewra water or essence and is used in sweet dishes. *Pandan* leaves can be bought from Asian grocers.

PRAWNS, DRIED See Shrimps, Dried.

RICE Most recipes call for 'fragrant' rice, which is long grain. Good quality, white long-grain rice can be used. The older and drier the rice the more water it will need to cook in, so always check when cooking the rice that it is not too dry. Always wash rice until the water runs clear; this rids it of dust, dirt and starch and begins the softening process.

Some recipes call for 'sticky' or 'glutinous' rice and, if you can't find it in a Thai shop, it is best to look for Italian, arborio or medium round-grain rice. Powdered, toasted (or ground, browned) rice is used in some dishes to give texture. For this you need to dry-fry raw long-grain rice until it is well browned and then grind it finely in a pestle and mortar.

RICE WRAPPERS OR PAPERS These are round, thin and brittle pancakes or crepes. They must be moistened with water before use to make them flexible. They are used in many ways to wrap food and make little parcels. Available in packets from Thai and Oriental stores.

SHRIMP PASTE Made from prawns and salt that have been allowed to ferment and then mashed to a paste. Can be bought in Oriental stores. This is very pungent and salty and used in small amounts. Anchovy paste could sometimes be used as a substitute. Some recipes call for it to be crushed with spices to make a paste which is then sautéed.

SHRIMPS, DRIED Also called dried prawns, these are available from Oriental stores in whole or powdered form. They are strongly flavoured, but milder than dried shrimp paste. To use whole ones, rinse briefly to get rid of dirt or grit.

SHALLOTS The best and most authentic type to use in the recipes in this book is the small red variety usually found in Chinese or Thai shops; they have a stronger flavour than normal onions. If they are not available then use European shallots or small onions.

SOY BEAN PASTE A Japanese seasoning mix made from fermented soy beans. There are different varieties depending on what has been added to the soy bean, for example: rice miso, kome-miso, barley miso/mugi-miso, and ordinary soy bean miso/mame-miso. Available in Oriental stores.

Soy Sauce Made from fermented soy beans, wheat flour, water and salt, soy sauce has a high salt content – not good for your blood pressure! There are two main types of soy sauce:

Light Obviously, light in colour but full of flavour, it is saltier than the dark variety and best used in cooking.

Dark This is aged much longer than light soy sauce, hence its darker colour. It is a little thicker and stronger too and is better for dipping sauces, and for adding colour to dishes as well as flavour.

Most soy sauces sold in supermarkets are the dark version, but Chinese stores sell both and usually the more authentic brands.

Star Anise This spice has a pungent liquorice taste that is used to add flavour to meat and poultry.

Stocks For the stocks in the soup recipes, you could use either the ready-made liquid variety available in tubs from many chain stores and supermarkets (watch when you season as they can be quite salty) or, better still, make your own. The recipes are on page 200. For chicken stock follow the Thai Soup Stock recipe and use chicken bones or carcasses.

Tamarind Now you will be interested to know that tamarind is the dried fruit of the tamarind tree, native to East Africa. It is sometimes called an Indian date because the tree is grown all over India and the fruit has a sticky appearance. It has a sharp, acidic taste. The pods are allowed to mature on the tree until the flesh turns dark brown and soft. They are then shelled and maybe seeded and sold in sticky brown blocks of tamarind pulp, which has to be made into tamarind water before using. To do this you have to soak 25g/1oz pulp in 300ml (½ pint) hot water, stir and leave for between 5–30 minutes. The longer the tamarind is left to soak, the stronger the flavour. The amount of tamarind pulp and water can be adjusted to the thickness required for the recipe. The tamarind water is strained off pressing as much out of the pulp as possible. The pulp is discarded.

Tamarind paste or concentrate is available from Asian stores and is ready to use. It is simply mixed with stock or water or even added directly to the dish. It does not need straining and again may be used in different strengths according to the recipe.

Tamarind syrup is sometimes required for recipes and can be bought in Oriental or specialist stores.

TANG CHI This is preserved radish, sold whole or in slices in vacuum-sealed packs. It is used chopped small, to add texture and flavour. Available from Chinese or Oriental stores.

TARO A starchy, bland flavoured tuber, this is peeled and then sliced or chopped before using. A potato may be used as a substitute.

TURMERIC This is another member of the ginger family and can sometimes be found fresh in Oriental stores or large supermarkets. Fresh turmeric has a brownish skin and a vivid, orangey flesh. Like fresh root ginger, it is used peeled and grated or finely chopped. More often, though, turmeric is found in its dried ground form. It is a bright yellow powder and has a hot flavour.

WHITE VINEGAR Use distilled malt vinegar, cider vinegar or preferably rice vinegar from Chinese stores.

ZERUMBET Widely cultivated throughout Asia, this variety of ginger is more bitter than the ordinary kind. The roots and rhizome are gigantic. Probably difficult to obtain here, so use normal fresh root ginger instead.

Although I and a team of culinary geniuses have checked every recipe in this book, please take all cooking times, oven temperatures, guides to the number of people a dish serves and measurements with a pinch of salt. No oven thermostat is identical, scales are sometimes incorrect and clocks go wrong. Remember that a dish is ready when you are satisfied – not just because the recipe or clock says so! After all, Asian charcoal burners don't have thermostats.

Metric and Imperial measurements are given in the recipes, so you can use whichever one you prefer. But follow only one or the other as the amounts are not always interchangeable. Ideally, use the measurements as a guide only and go with whatever looks right and tastes good. And remember to taste the dish continuously at every stage.

SOUPS

Soups are an important part of the south-east Asian diet. They are eaten at any time of the day, from breakfast through to supper. They may be the only dish of a meal or they may be one of several.

As a general rule, soups start with a clear stock made from vegetables, poultry, fish or beef. In my experience of eating in the homes of ordinary families and of buying food from the street hawkers, chicken stock is the one most usually used as a base. The next most important ingredient is either rice or egg noodles; this provides the protein and bulk of the meal.

The other essential ingredients are the herbs and spices. Examples of spices are: ginger (the Asians are lucky, they have at least three varieties of ginger, after root ginger the most common one is called galangal and there is another known as zerumbet – the last-named is hotter than the ginger we have in Europe); fish sauce; palm sugar (demerara sugar is an acceptable substitute); tamarind concentrate; chillies; shallots and garlic. These are all used in varying degrees and strength, depending on how hot, sweet or sour you like your soup. And then come the herbs – for instance, coriander, mint and basil – that are chopped and strewn uncooked over each bowl of soup.

As with pasta in Italy and rice in India, the noodles and rice of south-east Asia form the staple diet. The addition of meat, fish or vegetables is a luxury dictated by economic circumstances. Once you have this basic understanding of the soup – and I repeat that the stock is rich, clear and spicy, and that there are lots of noodles or rice to give it bulk – you are then free to add slivers of chicken, pork or beef, shellfish or any combination you choose, as well as spring onions or green vegetables, anything from spinach to pak choy to broccoli or cabbage, as you will. Bear in mind that these green vegetables should not be overcooked; they should be crunchy. If you use greens with thick stems, trim the stalks so that they cook at the same rate as the leaves.

Really, there should be no specific quantities for these soups; everything depends on the size of the vessel you prepare them in. If you have a family of six you have a big pot, if there are two of you, a small pot. And you fill them both accordingly.

PRAWN SOUP – SPICY AND SOUR
Vietnam
PHOTOGRAPH OPPOSITE PAGE 64

SERVES 8

450g (1lb) raw tiger or large prawns, shelled and deveined

4 cloves garlic, finely chopped

150ml (5fl oz) fish sauce

Freshly ground black pepper

4 tablespoons vegetable oil

4 shallots, thinly sliced

6 blades of lemon grass (include the white bulb, crushed)

4 tablespoons palm or demerara sugar

2 large ripe tomatoes, skinned and chopped

½ ripe pineapple, peeled and cut into small chunks

A handful of canned bamboo shoots, drained and chopped (optional)

Approx. 1 litre (1¾ pints) water

4 tablespoons tamarind concentrate, dissolved in 150ml (¼ pint) warm water

2 teaspoons salt

2 tablespoons beansprouts

4 red chilli peppers, seeded and chopped

A handful of chopped fresh mint and a few slivers of spring onions, to garnish

Mix together the prawns, garlic and a little of the fish sauce. Season with pepper and leave to marinate for 30 minutes.

Heat the oil in a large pan, add the shallots and lemon grass, and quickly sauté, but do not brown them. Add the sugar and tomatoes and cook until they have slightly softened. Pop in the pineapple and bamboo shoots, if you are using them, and continue cooking for a few minutes. Give it all a really good stir.

Tip in the water and, when it is boiling, mix in the tamarind liquid, the remaining fish sauce and salt. Reduce the heat and simmer for a further 5 minutes.

Add the prawns, beansprouts and chillies and cook for about 3 minutes, until the prawns are tender. Discard the lemon grass blades. Serve scattered with the mint and spring onion.

HOT AND SOUR SEAFOOD SOUP
Vietnam

SERVES 4

1 litre (1¾ pints) chicken stock
1 blade of lemon grass, finely
   sliced
2.5cm (1 inch) galangal,
   thinly sliced
2–3 Kaffir lime leaves
450g (1lb) king prawns,
   shelled and deveined,
   leaving tail ends intact
425g (15oz) can straw
   mushrooms, drained and
   quartered

Fresh coconut slivers (from
   about ¼ coconut)
1 tablespoon lime juice
2 teaspoons fish sauce
2 teaspoons chilli paste
Bird's-eye chilli peppers,
   seeded and thinly sliced,
   and fresh coriander leaves,
   to garnish

Heat the chicken stock in a pan over a medium heat. Add the lemon grass, galangal and lime leaves. Bring to the boil and throw in the prawns, mushrooms and coconut. Simmer gently until the prawns turn pink and are tender.

Meanwhile, mix together the lime juice, fish sauce and chilli paste. Stir this mixture into the soup when the prawns are cooked. Heat through for a minute or two, then serve sprinkled with the chillies and coriander leaves.

HOT AND SOUR PRAWN SOUP
Thailand

SERVES 4

425ml (¾ pint) rich chicken
  stock
425ml (¾ pint) water
225g (8oz) raw prawns,
  deveined, shells removed
  and reserved, but tails left
  intact
2 blades of lemon grass,
  crushed
4 Kaffir lime leaves, fresh or
  dried
A couple of slices of fresh root
  ginger

60ml (2fl oz) fish sauce
60ml (2fl oz) lime juice
1 teaspoon chilli paste
2 cloves garlic, finely chopped
2 shallots, finely chopped
3 green chilli peppers, seeded
  and chopped
425g (15oz) can straw
  mushrooms, drained and
  sliced
A few slivers of fresh coconut
1 tablespoon chopped fresh
  coriander leaves

Put the chicken stock and water into a large pan, add the rinsed prawn shells, which will give the soup extra flavour, lemon grass, lime leaves and ginger and simmer for 20 minutes. Strain the stock. Return the stock to a pan and add the fish sauce, lime juice and chilli paste.

Bring to the boil and throw in the garlic and shallots, the chillies, mushrooms and coconut slivers. Cook gently for around 3 minutes.

Add the prawns and simmer slowly, uncovered, for 2–3 minutes, until the prawns turn pink. Serve garnished with coriander.

Opposite: Chilli Prawns (page 140)
Next page: **Centre** Chicken Curry with Coconut Cream and
Sweet Potatoes (page 168); **Right** Malaysian Cucumber Pickle
(page 199)

RICE SOUP WITH PRAWNS
Thailand

SERVES 4

500ml (16fl oz) water
2 celery stalks, chopped
Dash of light soy sauce
A little white pepper
100g (4oz) short-grain rice,
  steamed
2 tablespoons fish sauce

225g (8oz) raw prawns,
  shelled and deveined
A few slivers of garlic
2 tablespoons groundnut oil
Fresh coriander leaves, to
  garnish

Put the water in a large pan and add the celery, soy sauce and white pepper. Bring to the boil. Add the rice, fish sauce and the prawns. Bring to the boil and cook until the prawns are cooked, about 3 minutes. Keep warm while you quickly sauté the garlic in the oil until it is just golden.

Pour into individual bowls, sprinkle with the fried garlic and scatter over a few coriander leaves.

PS I know some people add five spice powder or MSG (monosodium glutamate) in Thai dishes like this one, but personally I don't approve. A dash of soy sauce is better.

Top Pineapple and Cucumber Sambal (page 21);
Centre Stir-fried Spinach with Garlic (page 190);
Bottom Tamarind Chicken (page 149)

CRAB AND ASPARAGUS SOUP
Vietnam

PHOTOGRAPH OPPOSITE PAGE 64

The French introduced asparagus to Vietnam; the Vietnamese
call it 'Western Bamboo'.

SERVES 4

500ml (16fl oz) chicken stock
½ teaspoon brown sugar
1–2 tablespoons fish sauce
Salt
1 tablespoon vegetable oil
2 cloves garlic, chopped
5 shallots, chopped
Freshly ground black pepper
1 egg, lightly beaten

225g (8oz) cooked white
   crabmeat
450g (1lb) cooked asparagus
   tips, chopped into 2.5cm (1
   inch) chunks, plus a little of
   the cooking liquid
Chopped fresh coriander
   and/or a little finely
   chopped spring onion, to
   garnish

In a large pan, bring the stock, sugar and most of the fish sauce to a
boil. Season with salt and simmer for a few minutes.

Meanwhile, heat the oil and stir-fry the garlic and shallots for about
5 minutes, until they are soft. Lift out, drain and add to the stock
together with the remaining fish sauce and black pepper to season.
Bring it to the boil, then lower the heat and add the egg. Stir gently and
cook for a minute.

Pop in the crabmeat and the asparagus with a little of its cooking
liquid. Cook gently until thoroughly warmed. Sprinkle with coriander
and/or spring onion, and a twist of black pepper.

CHICKEN SOUP
Malaysia

SERVES 4–6

2 litres (3½ pints) water
½ free-range chicken (about
    900g [2lb]), or 2 quarters
Salt
100g (4oz) long-grain rice
2 teaspoons groundnut oil

6 pieces of finely sliced fresh
    root ginger
Freshly ground black pepper
Squeeze of lemon
1 tablespoon finely chopped
    spring onion

Bring the water to the boil in a large pan and add the chicken. Cover and simmer for 30 minutes.

Remove the chicken and, when cool, cut away the flesh from the bones. Pop the bones back into the pan of stock and return to the heat. Cut the chicken flesh into small strips, sprinkle with salt and keep warm.

Rinse the rice and cook in the boiling stock together with the oil and ginger. Simmer until the rice is tender – about 12–15 minutes. Take out and discard the chicken bones and replace with the chicken strips. Season with pepper, squeeze in the lemon and heat through for a few minutes. Serve strewn with the spring onion.

CHICKEN SOUP WITH COCONUT, GINGER & LEMON GRASS
Thailand

SERVES 4

150ml (¼ pint) chicken stock
2 blades of lemon grass, chopped
4 Kaffir lime leaves, torn in half
5 thin slices of fresh root ginger
500ml (16fl oz) coconut milk
225g (8oz) boned and skinned free-range chicken breast, very thinly sliced

4 tablespoons fish sauce
1 tablespoon brown sugar
125ml (4fl oz) lime juice
1 teaspoon black chilli paste
2 tablespoons chopped fresh coriander leaves
5 green chilli peppers, seeded and finely chopped

First, put the stock, lemon grass, lime leaves and ginger in a large pan. Bring to the boil, stirring.

Now add the coconut milk, chicken, fish sauce and sugar and simmer until the chicken slices are tender, about 5–10 minutes.

Put the lime juice and chilli paste in the base of a large serving bowl. Mix them together. Pour the hot soup on top and sprinkle with the coriander and chillies.

CHICKEN SOUP WITH GREEN MANGO AND GINGER
Thailand

SERVES 4

Approx. 850ml (1½ pints) water
3 tablespoons fish sauce
1 tablespoon palm or demerara sugar, or to your taste
½ small free-range chicken (about 700g [1½lb]), cut into small pieces leaving bones attached
2 tablespoons finely chopped fresh root ginger – make sure it is as fleshy and fresh as possible

4 shallots, finely sliced
10 fresh green peppercorns, crushed
1 teaspoon shrimp paste
1 tablespoon chopped fresh coriander root
1 green mango, sliced
Chopped fresh coriander
2 spring onions, chopped

Put the water, fish sauce and sugar into a large pan. Bring to the boil and add the chicken pieces, half the ginger, shallots and peppercorns. Cover and simmer gently for 20–30 minutes, or until the chicken is tender. Throw in the shrimp paste, coriander root, mango and remaining ginger and simmer for a further 10 minutes or so. Serve the soup hot, sprinkled with coriander and spring onions.

CHICKEN AND SWEET TAMARIND SOUP
Malaysia

SERVES 4

2 tablespoons groundnut oil
450g (1lb) free-range chicken
  breast fillets, skinned and
  cut into bite-size pieces
2.5cm (1 inch) piece of fresh
  root ginger, grated
6 shallots, chopped
2–3 tomatoes, skinned and
  chopped
Salt

Freshly ground black pepper
1 litre (1¾ pints) chicken stock
225g (8 oz) pineapple, skinned
  and chopped
1 teaspoon sugar
1 tablespoon tamarind
  concentrate
Chopped fresh coriander and
  mint leaves, to garnish

Heat the oil in a large pan and fry the chicken until it is lightly browned. Pop in the ginger and shallots and cook for 3–4 minutes. Add the tomatoes, seasoning and chicken stock. Bring to the boil and simmer until the chicken is tender – about 20–30 minutes.

Throw in the pineapple and stir in the sugar and tamarind. Simmer a little longer so the fruit warms through and the flavours mix. Sprinkle with the herbs and serve.

HERBAL CHICKEN SOUP
Thailand

SERVES 4–6

1 litre (1¾ pints) chicken stock
1.1kg (2½lb) free-range
    chicken, flesh removed and
    cut into small pieces – or, if
    you don't want to rip your
    chicken to pieces, use boned,
    chopped chicken thighs or
    breast fillets (you'll need
    about 350–450g [12oz–1lb])
4–6 shallots, sliced
225g (8oz) pineapple or green
    mango, peeled and chopped
225g (8oz) pumpkin, peeled
    and chopped

2 dried red chilli peppers,
    crushed
1 large clove garlic, crushed
1 grilled tomato, chopped
Dash of fish sauce
2 tablespoons lime juice
2 tablespoons tamarind water

To garnish:
1 tablespoon chopped fresh
    basil leaves
2 red chilli peppers, shredded
1 blade of lemon grass, very
    thinly sliced

In a large pan bring the stock to the boil, then add the chicken, shallots,
pineapple or mango, whichever you are using, and pumpkin and cook,
covered, for 15 minutes. Then add the chillies, garlic, tomato, fish sauce,
lime juice and tamarind water. Cover and continue cooking for a further
20–30 minutes, or until the chicken is tender. Before serving, garnish
with the basil, chillies and lemon grass. Serve steaming hot.

CHICKEN AND COCONUT HOT SOUP
Thailand

If you happen to have coconut palms in your garden, then this dish is great fun because you use the water from the coconut for your stock, you garnish the finished soup with the spooned-out soft flesh of the nut itself, and you use the shell as a soup bowl. Of course, if you don't have your own coconut palm, proceed anyway and adapt the recipe as appropriate.

SERVES 4

1 tablespoon coconut or peanut oil
1 tablespoon green curry paste
1.2 litres (2 pints) thin coconut milk
4 Kaffir lime leaves
1 blade of lemon grass, chopped
2 teaspoons grated fresh zerumbet or root ginger
450g (1lb) free-range chicken breast fillets, cut into 1cm (½ inch) strips
50g (2oz) green beans, finely sliced

2 tablespoons fish sauce
½ teaspoon palm or demerara sugar, or to taste
1 tablespoon roughly chopped fresh holy basil leaves – or use ordinary sweet basil
1 tablespoon roughly chopped fresh coriander
2 teaspoons chopped red chilli peppers – if you don't like it hot, seed the chillies first
2 green coconuts, halved, flesh scooped out and chopped

Heat the oil in a large pan and stir in the green curry paste. Cook for half a minute to release the flavours. Pour in the coconut milk, lime leaves, lemon grass and zerumbet or root ginger. Bring to the boil.

Pop in the chicken and simmer, uncovered, until the chicken is tender, about 20 minutes. Stir in the green beans, fish sauce, sugar, basil, coriander, chillies and coconut flesh. Simmer for 3–4 minutes and serve.

MEATY CABBAGE ROLLS IN SOUP
Vietnam

PHOTOGRAPH OPPOSITE PAGE 64

SERVES 4–6

10 large green cabbage (like pak choy or Savoy) leaves, cut in half and tough parts removed

Approx. 1 litre (1¾ pints) vegetable or chicken stock

A bunch of spring onions (about 10) – just the green bits

White part of 1 spring onion, finely chopped

1 clove garlic, finely chopped

1½ tablespoons fish sauce

50g (2oz) minced lean beef

175g (6oz) minced lean pork

Freshly ground black pepper

Salt

Dash of light soy sauce

To serve:

100g (4oz) long-grain rice, cooked

1 spring onion and fresh coriander leaves, finely chopped (optional)

Cook the cabbage leaves in boiling stock for about 2–3 minutes, until soft but not overcooked. You may have to do this in batches. Lift out and set aside. Toss the green spring onion leaves into the stock for a few seconds only until just soft and pliable. Remove and drain. Keep the liquid to use later. Now slice the spring onion leaves in half lengthways to make the long thin strips you need to tie the parcels.

Mix together the spring onion, garlic, just a shake of the fish sauce and the minced beef and pork. Season with pepper. To mix, it really does work best if you use your hands.

Spoon a mound of the meat mixture on to each cabbage leaf, fold the sides into the centre and roll up to make a small parcel. Secure each package by tying a strand of spring onion round its middle.

Bring the reserved stock back to the boil, season with a little salt to taste, add the rest of the fish sauce and a dash of soy sauce. Carefully put in the cabbage rolls and cook for about 15 minutes, or until the stuffing is firm when tested with a sharp knife.

Put some rice in individual bowls, top with some cabbage rolls, then just cover with soup. Sprinkle with spring onion and coriander, if you like.

SPINACH AND BEEF SOUP
Vietnam

SERVES 4 GENEROUSLY

175g (6oz) fillet or sirloin
    steak, shredded
1 shallot, thinly sliced
2 cloves garlic, thinly sliced
3 tablespoons fish sauce
¼ teaspoon sugar
Freshly ground black pepper

1.2 litres (2 pints) water
Good bunch of spinach leaves
    (100g [4oz]), thoroughly
    washed and trimmed
1 tablespoon lemon juice
1 red chilli pepper, seeded and
    finely sliced

First, you need to marinate the beef with the shallot, garlic, a little of the fish sauce, sugar and black pepper. Cover and leave for at least 30 minutes.

Bring the water to the boil and add the rest of the fish sauce. Pop in the spinach and return to the boil. Add the meat and marinade, stir well and then turn off the heat. Stir in the lemon juice, twist on some black pepper to taste, sprinkle on the chilli and serve.

BEEF SOUP WITH LEMON GRASS
Vietnam

SERVES 4–6

175g (6oz) beef (fillet, sirloin
    or rump), thinly sliced
1 clove garlic, chopped
4 teaspoons fish sauce
Sprinkling of freshly ground
    black pepper
1 tablespoon vegetable oil

2 shallots, chopped
Blade of lemon grass, chopped
850ml (1½ pints) beef stock
Salt
1 tablespoon chopped fresh
    coriander leaves

Arrange the meat in a shallow dish, cover with the garlic, half the fish sauce and the black pepper. Leave to marinate for about an hour so the meat absorbs the flavours.

Cut the meat into strips. In a large pan or wok, heat the oil and stir-fry the shallots for 2–3 minutes. Throw in the lemon grass and cook for a minute. Add the meat and stir-fry over a high heat so it is well sealed. Cook for 2–3 minutes.

Pour in the beef stock and the remaining 2 teaspoons fish sauce and season to taste with salt. Bring to the boil. Scatter with coriander leaves and serve at once.

PHO

Vietnam

SERVES 6

450g (1lb) marrow bones
A few black peppercorns,
    crushed
Couple of star anise
Few whole cloves
2 onions, halved and grilled
    until burnt on the flat side
5cm (2 inch) piece of fresh root
    ginger, sliced
2 small white radish (Daikon
    or mooli), sliced
2 litres (3½ pints) water
225g (8oz) rice noodles,
    soaked in cold water for 10
    minutes and drained
225g (8oz) fillet of beef,
    shredded
6–8 spring onions, white part
    sliced, green part finely
    chopped

2 red chilli peppers, seeded
    and sliced
100g (4oz) beansprouts
1 free-range egg yolk per
    serving
Fresh mint leaves

For the garnish:
Chopped fresh mint and basil
    leaves
Chopped seeded chilli peppers
Chopped beansprouts

To serve:
Fish sauce
Soy bean paste (Miso)
Chilli sauce
Lime or lemon juice

To make the stock, brown the marrow bones in a roasting pan in a preheated oven, 200°C/400°F (gas mark 6), for about 30 minutes. Put the bones in a large pan together with the peppercorns, anise, whole cloves, onions, ginger, radish and water. Bring to the boil. Reduce the heat, cover and simmer for 2–3 hours, skimming off any fat or scum from the surface from time to time. Cool, then strain.

Cook the rice noodles in boiling water for 3–5 minutes. Drain and put into large individual soup bowls. Add some beef, spring onions, chillies and beansprouts to each bowl. Bring the stock to a fast rolling boil and pour it into the soup bowls. Add the egg yolk and mint leaves to each bowl.

Serve at once sprinkled with a garnish of your choice and add fish sauce etc., according to taste.

MEE SOUP
Malaysia

SERVES 6–8

4 tablespoons groundnut oil
4 shallots, sliced finely
2 cloves garlic
300g (11–12oz) cooked,
  shelled prawns
1 tablespoon black
  peppercorns, roughly
  crushed
1.5 litres (2½ pints) water
Salt
100g (4oz) pak choy or green
  cabbage, shredded

350g (12oz) beansprouts
2 beancurd cakes, each about
  7.5cm (3 inches), fried and
  cubed
600g (1¼lb) egg noodles
2 tomatoes, each cut into 6

For the garnish:
6 tiny hot red chilli peppers,
  seeded and thinly sliced
1 large onion, sliced thinly
2 tablespoons dark soy sauce

Heat the oil in a large pan and fry the shallots and garlic for about 5 minutes, until soft. Stir in the prawns and the pepper and mix well. Pour in the water and bring to the boil. Season to taste. Cook for 3–4 minutes.

Add the pak choy or cabbage, beansprouts and fried beancurd. Cook for about 5 minutes. Pop in the noodles and tomatoes. Cook for 1 minute.

To make the garnish, simply mix together the three ingredients, and serve it with the Mee Soup.

FISH
AND SHELLFISH

SAUTÉED FILLET OF SOLE WITH GREEN
VEGETABLES IN BLACK BEAN SAUCE
Hong Kong

PHOTOGRAPH OPPOSITE PAGE 96

Don't be put off by the thought of eating cooked fish bones. As long as you have cooked them until they are really, really crispy, you can munch them rather like the deep-fried Bombay duck you have in Indian restaurants. I can assure you that when my Chinese chums at the Mandarin Oriental Hotel in Hong Kong cooked me this, it was delicious.

SERVES 2

1kg (2–2¼lb) Dover sole, or two smaller ones
A little plain flour
Sunflower or groundnut oil for deep-frying
Cornflour
1 teaspoon egg white
1 teaspoon chopped fresh root ginger
1 teaspoon finely chopped garlic

1 teaspoon black bean paste
½ teaspoon finely chopped tangerine peel
4 tablespoons chicken stock
2 tablespoons rice wine or dry sherry
A pinch of sugar
A pinch of salt
1 teaspoon oyster sauce
½ teaspoon black bean sauce

Carefully fillet the sole (or, better still, ask your fishmonger to skin and fillet it for you), keeping the skeleton of the fish in one piece. Dust the skeleton with plain flour and deep-fry in about 2.5–5cm (1–2 inches) hot oil until crisp and golden brown – about 3–4 minutes. The skeleton should be very crisp so that it can be eaten. The Chinese really like this – I've tried it and it *is* good. Drain on kitchen paper and keep warm.

Skin the fillets of sole. Cut the fish into 2.5cm (1 inch) strips and mix with a generous sprinkling of cornflour and a little egg white. Deep-fry the fish pieces in 2.5cm (1 inch) hot oil for 1 minute. Drain thoroughly.

Heat 2 tablespoons oil in a wok or frying pan and sauté the ginger, garlic, black bean paste and tangerine peel for a couple of minutes.

Add the stock and rice wine or sherry. Pop in the sugar, salt and oyster and black bean sauces. Stir well. Mix ½ teaspoon cornflour with 1 tablespoon water, then stir this into the sauce. Cook, stirring until thickened, add the pieces of sole and cook quickly until hot.

Pile the sole on to the crisp fried skeleton and serve at once.

REMPAH FISH
Malaysia

Now, my little gastronauts, I am sure you will have read previously in this tome that the preparation of the curry paste known as *rempah* is considered to be a highly esteemed work of art, so do take great care to make it well.

But if you have got this far into the book, you might well have decided that your next holidays must be spent in the East, and so you have probably taken a part-time job to save enough pennies to go, and you don't really have very much time free. Therefore, under Article 37 of the Floyd Cooks' Code (1991) you are permitted, under such exceptional circumstances, to pop into your Asian food store and buy some pre-prepared Thai red curry paste.

SERVES 4

To make Malaysian *rempah* you will need:

2 tablespoons finely chopped fresh root ginger	6 shallots, finely chopped
4 blades of lemon grass, finely chopped	30–40 small red chilli peppers, seeded and chopped
3–4 cloves garlic, finely chopped	1 teaspoon black peppercorns, crushed
24 roasted peanuts, or cashews or almonds, chopped	1 teaspoon brown sugar
	1 teaspoon ground turmeric
	3 teaspoons salt

Pop all the above ingredients into a food processor, or use a pestle and mortar, and grind until you have a smooth paste. This will make enough to store for future use. It is extremely hot, so use sparingly.

To make Rempah Fish you will need:

1 tablespoon fish paste
1 red chilli pepper, seeded and
very finely chopped
450g (1lb) firm white fish
fillets, such as cod, halibut
or haddock
Vegetable oil for frying
1 onion, grated
4 Kaffir lime leaves
300ml (½ pint) water

2 tablespoons rempah *or red*
curry paste
1 teaspoon fennel seeds
1 teaspoon cumin seeds
1 tablespoon coriander seeds,
crushed
4 spring onions, finely sliced
1 clove garlic, finely sliced
Lime juice

Right, first mix together the fish paste and chilli and spread over the fish fillets. Cut the fish into slices.

Heat 2 tablespoons oil in a pan and sauté the onion for 5 minutes, until softened. Add the lime leaves, water and *rempah* or red curry paste. Bring to the boil, stirring. Throw in the fennel, cumin and coriander seeds. Simmer for about 7 minutes so that you have a delicious coating for the fish. Crisp fry the spring onions and garlic in a little oil. Put to one side.

In a separate pan or a wok, fry the sliced fish in a little oil for 2–3 minutes, until it is tender. Drain off the oil, pour over the sauce and simmer gently for a couple of minutes until it is heated through. Add lime juice to taste and garnish with the spring onion and garlic.

BASS WITH GARLIC SAUCE
Thailand

A hotel in Bangkok runs a Thai cookery course for visitors and locals alike. It doesn't go to great lengths but it provides a useful insight into Thai cooking. The presentation was made by a rather zappy young man who looked like a hair salon proprietor, behaved like a DJ and spoke with a dead cool American accent.

I cooked him this dish, which my chum Chom had taught me, by way of a 'thank you for letting us mess up your lecture this morning'.

SERVES 2–3

1 whole bass, grouper or
   mullet (at least 450g [1lb]),
   scaled, gutted and cleaned
50g (2oz) plain flour
1 litre (1¾ pints) vegetable oil
1 whole head garlic (a little
   less if you prefer), chopped
1 generous tablespoon
   chopped spring onion
2 tablespoons seeded and
   chopped mixed red and
   green chilli peppers

1 teaspoon ground coriander
3 tablespoons brown sugar
2 tablespoons lime juice
1 tablespoon lemon juice
90ml (3fl oz) fish sauce
1 tablespoon chopped fresh
   basil
White pepper

Wash and dry the fish. With a sharp knife make half a dozen slashes over the skin of the fish on each side. Dredge with flour on both sides for a non-stick fish with crispy skin.

Find a deepish pan big enough to hold the whole fish and the oil. Heat the oil, bar about 3 tablespoons, and cook the fish for around 5 minutes. Turn it with care and fry for another 5 minutes. The flesh should be firm but still moist and tender. Remove the fish – again with care, so it doesn't break – drain and keep warm on a large serving dish.

Heat the remaining 3 tablespoons oil in a medium pan. Stir in the garlic, spring onion, chillies and coriander and cook gently for 2–3 minutes. Stir in the sugar, lime and lemon juices, fish sauce and basil. Simmer for about 2 minutes, stirring. Season with pepper. Pour over the fish and the dish is ready to serve.

STEAMED BASS OR GROUPER WITH CHILLI SAUCE

Thailand

CENTRE-SPREAD PHOTOGRAPH BETWEEN PAGES 64 AND 65

A firm fish like bass, or mullet, is perfect for steaming – and especially with these tangy flavours from the herbs and spices. The steaming process really does enhance the flavours.

SERVES 4

1 or 2 whole bass or grouper (weighing 700g [1½lb]), scaled, gutted and cleaned

2 tablespoons rice wine (or use dry sherry)

4 green chilli peppers, seeded and finely chopped

2 spring onions, very finely chopped

2 cloves garlic, crushed or finely chopped

2 tablespoons grated fresh root ginger

1 small onion, thinly sliced

2 blades of lemon grass, crushed and finely chopped

3 tablespoons fish sauce

60ml (2fl oz) lime juice

2 tablespoons chopped fresh basil

Salt

White pepper

Wash and dry the fish. With a sharp knife make half-a-dozen slashes over the skin of the fish. Mix together all the remaining ingredients and spread over the fish. Steam on a perforated tray in a large wok that has a domed lid for about 25 minutes, or until the flesh is firm but still moist and tender. Alternatively, you could use a big bamboo steamer or a fish kettle. To serve, pass round the chilli sauce separately.

CHILLI SAUCE

10 green chilli peppers, seeded and chopped

4 cloves garlic, chopped

120ml (4fl oz) fish sauce

150ml (5fl oz) lime or lemon juice

Put the four ingredients in your blender or food processor and whizz well. It's as easy as that!

FRIED FISH AND GINGER
Thailand
PHOTOGRAPH OPPOSITE PAGE 97

To my mind, bass is undoubtedly the king of fish, and a whole, crispy, deep-fried one is a gourmet's treat. But this dish would work equally well with inexpensive dabs or soles. The trick is to drizzle hot oil on to the ginger and spring onions so that they actually cook very lightly.

SERVES 4

2 tablespoons Chinese or ordinary brandy
1 tablespoon light soy sauce
1 teaspoon brown sugar
1 tablespoon sesame oil
1 or 2 whole bass or grey mullet (weighing 900g [2lb]), scaled, gutted and cleaned
A little plain flour

Groundnut or sunflower oil for frying, about 150ml (¼ pint)
1 tablespoon fresh root ginger, shredded
2 tablespoons shredded spring onions
1 red chilli pepper, seeded and finely sliced

Mix together the brandy, soy sauce, sugar and sesame oil. With a sharp knife make several diagonal slashes on both sides of the bass. Lay the fish in a dish and pour over the marinade. Leave in a cool place for about an hour.

Drain the fish and dredge well with flour. Heat the oil until sizzling in a large wok or deep pan. Fry the fish for about 15–20 minutes, until crisp and tender. Carefully lift out the fish and place on a serving dish.

Sprinkle over the ginger and spring onions. Take some hot oil from the wok and drizzle 3 or 4 tablespoons of it over the ginger and spring onions. Garnish with the chilli.

TURMERIC FISH
Thailand

We had this for lunch on the beach of one of the small islands off Ko Samui. The joy of it was, we had caught the mackerel ourselves, we had fresh turmeric root and we also had banana leaves. I just cooked the fish in the embers of a wood fire for about ten minutes.

SERVES 4

2 cloves garlic, crushed
1 tablespoon ground turmeric
  (if you can find fresh
  turmeric grate it very
  finely)
Salt

12 white peppercorns, crushed
4 whole mackerel, cleaned and
  gutted
Banana leaves or baking
  parchment
Aluminium foil

Mix together the garlic, turmeric, salt and pepper. Rub the fish well with the mixture. Wrap in a banana leaf or parchment and then in aluminium foil. Bake in a preheated oven, 200°C/400°F (gas mark 6), for about 20–30 minutes, or until tender. These fish parcels will taste even better cooked over a charcoal barbecue.

SQUID IN MILD CURRY SAUCE
Malaysia

This fiery yet creamy curry is a perfect example of a
thoroughbred Malay dish.

SERVES 4

2–3 shallots, chopped
1½ teaspoons finely chopped
  garlic
1 teaspoon shrimp paste
8 dried red chilli peppers,
  soaked and seeded
2 tablespoons ground
  coriander
2½ teaspoons ground cumin
45g (1½oz) desiccated
  coconut
½ teaspoon ground turmeric

3 tablespoons coconut or
  peanut oil
6 slices of fresh root ginger
1 blade of lemon grass, halved
  lengthways
3 Kaffir lime leaves
500ml (16fl oz) thick coconut
  milk
Salt
Freshly ground black pepper
700g (1½lb) squid, cleaned,
  rinsed, scored and cut into
  squares

Using a pestle and mortar or blender, grind the shallots, garlic, shrimp paste, chillies, coriander, cumin, desiccated coconut and turmeric to a paste.

Heat the oil in a wok or pan and gently fry this seasoning paste for 3 minutes. Pop in the ginger, lemon grass, lime leaves, coconut milk and seasoning to taste. Bring to the boil, then reduce the heat and cook, stirring for 3–4 minutes.

Add the squid and cook gently for 5 minutes, until the squid is slightly firmer and cooked. The squid needs very little cooking or it can become rubbery.

FISH STEAMED WITH CELERY
Thailand

This is a fine way of injecting some flavour into the humbler species of fish like whiting or small pollock. But if the pocket permits, go for bass or red mullet.

SERVES 2–3

5 stalks of celery
1 whole saltwater fish (550g [1¼lb]), whiting, pollock, bass or red mullet, scaled, cleaned and gutted
Salt
Freshly ground black pepper

2 green chilli peppers, seeded and finely chopped
2 cloves garlic, finely chopped
4 spring onions, finely chopped
1 tablespoon fish sauce
1 wineglass dry white wine

It is important first to remove the 'strings' from the celery, so there are no fibrous bits on the outside. Cut the celery into thin strips about 7.5cm (3 inches) long. Be careful not to cut the celery too coarsely or it will take longer to cook than the fish.

With a sharp knife, make several deep slashes on each side of the fish, then rub in the salt and pepper. Put the fish in a steamer or fish kettle, add the celery, then sprinkle and pour on the remaining ingredients. You could also steam the fish on a perforated tray in a large wok with a lid. Steam until the fish is firm but still moist, about 15 minutes.

HOT AND SOUR FISH
Vietnam

On one of our trips from Saigon, we went to a charming fishing village
called Long Hai, where we stayed in a Vietnamese Government-run
hotel. It was a mock French château built in the late 1940s by a million-
aire. He needed a remote hideaway for his daughter, who had leprosy.
Today it has been stripped of its former finery and has all the comforts
of the sort of hostel that I imagine George Orwell stayed in when he
was researching *Down and Out in Paris and London*!
From the roof of the hotel there was a spectacular view of the little
town, very French in style (in colonial times it was a holiday resort),
and of the long, curving beach, where each morning just after dawn
the fishing fleet unloaded their catch for the market, which was held
on the beach. It was on the same roof, one sunny morning, that I
prepared the following dish.

SERVES 4

For the fish stock:
450g (1lb) fish trimmings,
    heads, tails, bones, etc.
1 onion, chopped
1 carrot, chopped
2 stalks of celery, chopped
A few white peppercorns
2.5cm (1 inch) piece of fresh
    root ginger, chopped
2 cloves garlic, crushed or
    finely chopped
2–3 star anise
25g (1oz) tamarind pulp,
    soaked in 300ml (½ pint)
    water for 10 minutes,
    squeezed, strained and
    water retained
1 litre (1¾ pints) water

Vegetable oil for deep-frying
450g (1lb) fish fillets, such as
    mackerel or red snapper,
    sliced

225g (8oz) okra or green beans
    or baby green aubergines,
    chopped
225g (8oz) ripe tomatoes,
    quartered
1–2 red chilli peppers, seeded
    and chopped
2 slices ripe pineapple,
    roughly chopped
A few slices of taro or white
    radish
Fresh coriander leaves
Fresh basil leaves
Some curry leaves
Minced and deep-fried onion
    and garlic, to garnish

Put all the stock ingredients into a large pan. Bring to the boil, then reduce the heat. Cover and simmer very gently for 30 minutes. Cool slightly, then strain through a fine sieve back into the pan. Boil the fish stock and pour into a hot steamer or a pan over which you can set a bamboo steamer.

Heat about 2.5cm (1 inch) oil in a wok or deep pan and fry the slices of fish, a few at a time, for 3–4 minutes only so they remain whole and firm when cooked.

Put the okra or whatever you are using, tomatoes, chillies, pineapple and taro or radish into the top half of the steamer, about 5–8 minutes before serving so that they cook very slightly and remain crunchy.

Add the deep-fried fish pieces and scatter the herbs on top.

Heat for about 5 minutes and lift out on to one large serving dish or individual plates. Garnish with the deep-fried onion and garlic.

FRIED MUSSELS
Thailand

CENTRE-SPREAD PHOTOGRAPH BETWEEN PAGES 96 AND 97

These simple, spicy mussels are finger-lickin', dead good! I bought a bowl of them from a floating kitchen set up in a little twelve-foot punt, as I was paddling around the Bangkok Floating Market on Sunday morning, as one does.

SERVES 2–3

3 tablespoons groundnut oil
3 shallots, finely chopped
3 cloves garlic, finely chopped
1 tablespoon soy bean paste
1 red chilli pepper, seeded and chopped

2.5cm (1 inch) piece of fresh root ginger, chopped
700g (1½lb) mussels in shells, cleaned, bearded and rinsed
1 teaspoon brown sugar

Heat the oil in a large pan and lightly brown the shallots and garlic for around 5 minutes. Add the soy bean paste and mix this in well before adding the chilli, ginger and mussels. Stir-fry these over a high heat for a minute before sprinkling on the sugar.

Cover the pan and cook over a high heat for about 5 minutes, shaking the pan frequently until the mussels have opened and released their juices. Discard any that remain obstinately shut or you may regret it.

Transfer the mussels to individual bowls and strain over the cooking liquid.

SWEET AND SOUR PRAWNS
Hong Kong

This is the dish I cooked at the fishing village of Sai Kung in the New Territories, where the obnoxious water-taxi driver caused so much trouble (see page 46).

SERVES 4

450g (1lb) raw tiger prawns, shelled, deveined and tails left intact
50g (2oz) plain flour
¼ teaspoon salt
Freshly ground black pepper
1 litre (1¾ pints) groundnut or sunflower oil
2 red peppers, seeded and finely sliced
1 red chilli pepper, seeded and finely sliced
1 teaspoon rice wine or dry sherry
225ml (8fl oz) ready-prepared sweet and sour sauce – buy it from your local Oriental store or supermarket
1 teaspoon sugar
1 teaspoon sesame oil
1 teaspoon cornflour
1 tablespoon water

Slash along the back of each prawn, then wash and dry them. Mix together the flour, salt and pepper. Dredge the prawns in the seasoned flour and then deep-fry them in about 2.5cm (1 inch) of hot oil until golden. If you are using a wok, you will need to fry them in small batches. Drain well.

Heat a couple of tablespoons oil in a wok or frying pan. Cook the peppers and chilli together for 2–3 minutes. Add the rice wine or sherry and sweet and sour sauce. Season to taste with sugar and pepper and bring to the boil. Mix together the oil, cornflour and water and add to the sauce. Stir until thickened.

Toss the prawns back into the pan and heat through, stirring, for 1–2 minutes before serving.

CHILLI PRAWNS
Malaysia

PHOTOGRAPH OPPOSITE PAGE 112

Prawns come in all shapes and sizes in Malaysia, from shrimp-size ones as small as your fingernail to monsters about a foot long. They are cheap and plentiful and I particularly enjoyed this little snack that my friend chef Razak prepared for me one breakfast-time in the Tanjong Jara beach resort.

SERVES 4

4 tablespoons groundnut oil
1 tablespoon grated onion
1 tablespoon minced or grated
   fresh root ginger
1 small onion, chopped
2 shallots, chopped
At least 450g (1lb) tomatoes,
   skinned and chopped

Pinch of ground saffron
1 tablespoon chilli sauce
1 tablespoon hot chilli sauce
1 tablespoon ground turmeric
700g (1½lb) large cooked
   prawns, peeled and heads
   removed, tails left intact
Cucumber, sliced or cubed

Heat half the oil in a pan. Add the grated onion, ginger, chopped onion and shallots and cook gently for around 10 minutes. Pop in the tomatoes, saffron and chilli sauces and cover. Cook for about 15 minutes.

Sprinkle the turmeric over the prawns. Heat the remaining oil in a wok or frying pan and fry the prawns briskly for about 2 minutes. Drain and arrange on a serving dish. Add a little water to the sauce if necessary to give a pouring consistency. Heat through, then pour over the prawns or serve separately and garnish with the cucumber.

CHILLI CRABS
Malaysia

I prepared this dish in the courtyard of a Portuguese restaurant in Malacca, where flat blue Swimmer crabs with quite soft shells are much prized. But there is no reason why you shouldn't use our regular English crabs or Dublin Bay prawns or lobsters or crayfish. It is another of those dishes you eat with your fingers.

This recipe leaves the crabmeat inside the shell. If you don't want the bother of digging out the crabmeat when you are eating this dish use cooked crabmeat flesh instead.

SERVES 4

1 blade of lemon grass, chopped
10 shallots, chopped
6 cloves garlic, chopped
5cm (2 inch) piece of fresh root ginger, chopped
2.5cm (1 inch) piece of fresh turmeric, chopped or 1 teaspoon dried turmeric
1 tablespoon fish paste
15 dried red chilli peppers

3 tablespoons groundnut oil
2 tablespoons tamarind pulp, mixed with 4 tablespoons water, and strained
Salt and brown sugar to taste
Water
900g (2lb) crabs, boiled, cleaned and each body cut into 2 or 4 pieces, depending on size

Using a pestle and mortar or blender, grind the lemon grass, shallots, garlic, ginger, turmeric, fish paste and chillies to make a paste.

Heat the oil in a frying pan or wok and fry the spice paste for 1 minute, stirring all the time, to release the flavours and make it more mellow.

Add the tamarind juice, salt and sugar, then pour in a little water. Bring to the boil and gently stir in the crabs. Simmer for 5 minutes, stirring constantly. The crabs should be hot and well coated and the dish should be on the dry side without too much sauce.

LOBSTER IN PRESERVED BLACK BEAN SAUCE

Hong Kong

CENTRE-SPREAD PHOTOGRAPH BETWEEN PAGES 96 AND 97

On a stormy day in Aberdeen Harbour, Hong Kong, in a rocking sampan that made us all feel sick and meant that Paul could hardly hold the camera straight, I was obliged to prepare a meal for a local hero – an inventor of sex games, foodwriter, philosopher, martial arts expert, television horse-racing tipster, journalist and actor – who goes by the name of Zachary Ulysses Greenstreet Octavius Kan. With his shaven head, he sat benignly radiating calm in the midst of the confusion that surrounded the cooking of this dish.

Ideally, you should use a live lobster for this recipe, but as these can be difficult to obtain, here is a version using cooked lobster. If you can find a live lobster, you will need to kill it first by plunging it into boiling water. It will squeak. Cook until it turns red – about 5–10 minutes. Drain and proceed as below.

SERVES 1–2

1 tablespoon ginger wine or dry sherry
1 tablespoon cornflour
Freshly ground black pepper
1 cooked lobster about 900g (2lb), washed and cut into small pieces, shell left on
1 litre (1¾ pints) groundnut or sunflower oil
1 teaspoon minced root ginger
2 cloves garlic, minced or finely chopped
2 tablespoons preserved black bean paste

2 green peppers, seeded and cut into 1cm (½ inch) squares
3 red chilli peppers, seeded and thinly sliced
1 teaspoon rice wine or dry sherry
125ml (4fl oz) fish or vegetable stock
3 tablespoons light soy sauce
3 teaspoons sugar
2 spring onions, sliced

Mix together the ginger wine or sherry, cornflour and a large pinch of pepper. Coat the lobster pieces with this mixture. Heat the oil and deep-fry the lobster pieces for 1–2 minutes. Lift out and drain. Heat 3 tablespoons oil in a wok or frying pan and sauté the ginger and garlic for a couple of minutes. Stir in the black bean paste, green peppers and chillies, mixing well.

Return the lobster pieces to the pan with the wine or sherry, stock and seasonings. Cover and simmer for 2–5 minutes. Finally, toss in the spring onions before serving.

FRIED CRAB WITH CHILLI PASTE
Thailand

The egg mixture in this dish makes a pleasing change. Be sure to make a fairly thin omelette mix, so that it coats the crabs like a batter.

SERVES 4

2 tablespoons vegetable oil	2 tablespoons chilli oil
4 live soft-shelled blue crabs	1 teaspoon sugar
or 450g (1lb) cooked	2 teaspoons light soy sauce
crabmeat	2 stalks of celery, sliced
2 cloves garlic, crushed	2 spring onions, sliced
2 shallots, chopped	1–2 red chilli peppers, seeded
3 eggs, beaten	and sliced
2 tablespoons chilli paste	

Heat the oil in a large, lidded sauté or frying pan. Add the crabs, garlic and shallots and cook until the top of the crab shells and the claws have turned red. If using crabmeat heat it through for 1–2 minutes. Cover with the lid and finish cooking. Beat together the eggs, chilli paste, chilli oil, sugar and soy sauce. Pour the egg mixture over the crabs and cook until the eggs have set softly around the crab pieces. Cover again for a minute so the top sets. Finally, just before serving, stir in the celery, spring onions and chillies.

Opposite: Rice in Banana Leaves with Coconut Sambal
(page 180)
Next page: **Left** Pork and Prawn Stew (page 162); **Right** Sticky Rice
with Chicken and Pork (page 177)

SEARED SCALLOPS AND SPRING ONIONS

Hong Kong

I cooked this dish for the chefs of the Hong Kong Mandarin, and if you ever find yourself there, ask them to show you the kitchen. Massive gas rings roar like dragons and have the power of 747 turbo jets. Dishes like this one really do take only seconds to prepare on that kind of cooking equipment.

SERVES 1–2

1 tablespoon vegetable oil
6 scallops – buy them ready cleaned
4 spring onions, cut into 2.5cm (1 inch) pieces
1 tablespoon finely chopped garlic
1 tablespoon finely chopped fresh root ginger

1 tablespoon shredded, seeded red chilli peppers
1 tablespoon shredded carrot
50g (2oz) green peppers, seeded and cut into 1cm (½ inch) pieces
Dash of dark soy sauce

Heat the oil in a wok and sear the scallops for around 5–8 minutes, until they become opaque and slightly golden, then remove.

Throw the spring onions, garlic, ginger, chillies, carrot and green peppers into the wok and stir-fry for 5 seconds over a high heat. Replace the scallops. Stir briefly and add the soy sauce. Toss well together and serve.

Fried Beef with Cashew Nuts (page 161)

THAI FISH CAKES AND CUCUMBER SALAD
Thailand

A perfect light lunch or supper with an authentic taste of Thailand that is easy to prepare.

MAKES ABOUT 10–12

450g (1lb) skinned fillets of firm white fish, such as cod or haddock
1–2 tablespoons red curry paste
1 egg, beaten
2 teaspoons fish sauce

A handful of Kaffir lime leaves and basil leaves, finely chopped
A little plain flour for dredging
Groundnut or sunflower oil for deep-frying

Put the fish, curry paste and egg into a food processor and whizz until smooth. Add the fish sauce and whizz again – don't let the mixture become too runny. Add the lime and basil leaves.

With your hands form the mixture into small cakes about 5cm (2 inches) wide. Dredge well with flour. Deep-fry in a wok in 2.5cm (1 inch) hot oil for a few minutes until crisp and golden.

CUCUMBER SALAD

1 cucumber, peeled, seeded and grated
2–3 red chilli peppers, seeded and chopped
2–3 shallots, grated

2 tablespoons fish sauce
2 tablespoons dried prawn powder
Juice of half a lemon or lime

Put all the ingredients into a bowl, mix well together and serve.

DEEP-FRIED PRAWN CAKES
Thailand

Just a more expensive variation of the preceding recipe.

MAKES ABOUT 15–20

450g (1lb) cooked prawns,
  shelled
1–2 tablespoons red curry
  paste
1 egg, beaten

1 tablespoon fish sauce
25g (1oz) cornflour
Groundnut or sunflower oil
  for deep-frying

Put the prawns, red curry paste, egg and fish sauce into a food processor and whizz until smooth.

With your hands shape the mixture into about 15–20 tiny cakes and roll in the cornflour.

Deep-fry in 2.5 cm (1 inch) hot oil for about 2 minutes, until the prawn cakes are golden brown and delicious.

SAMUI OYSTER FONDUE
Thailand
PHOTOGRAPH OPPOSITE PAGE 65

This fondue has nothing to do with Swiss fondues. This one necessitates cooking the ingredients in a steamboat – an Asian fondue set. Steamboats are round with a chimney or funnel in the centre surrounded by a deep 'moat'. The pan is heated over a charcoal burner or gas fire. The heat rises up the chimney, the sides of which heat the moat containing the liquid or stock for cooking. The ingredients are dipped into the hot stock, using chopsticks or wire mesh baskets, until they are cooked. You can buy steamboats from large Chinese stores (the kind that sell equipment too) in most cities.

For the stock:
1.2 litres (2 pints) water
1 blade of lemon grass, crushed
15g (½oz) flaked Katsuobushi (*dried flaked bonito fish*)
2.5cm (1 inch) piece of galangal, chopped
Salt
2 fresh coriander roots
3–4 Kaffir lime leaves, crushed
1 bulb garlic, cloves separated and peeled

2–3 tablespoons pickled cabbage

For the garlic and chilli sauce:
1 tablespoon fish sauce
1 teaspoon brown sugar
2 tablespoons lime juice
3 cloves garlic, coarsely chopped
2 bird's-eye chilli peppers, seeded and chopped
1 tablespoon chopped fresh coriander leaves

Plump, fresh oysters

To make the stock, put all the ingredients into a pan, half cover with a lid and simmer gently for 30 minutes. Transfer the stock to a steamboat or a flameproof pan set over a hot plate (the burner on a fondue set does not bring the stock to boiling point).

Next, make the sauce: mix together all the ingredients in a bowl.

To open the oysters, stick a strong knife into the back of each one near where the muscle holds the shells together, slice the muscle and prise open the shell.

Arrange the opened oysters on a dish. At table dip the oysters into the hot stock to cook quickly. Then dip into the sauce. The stock is then eaten as a soup later.

CHICKEN

TAMARIND CHICKEN
Malaysia

PHOTOGRAPH OPPOSITE PAGE 113

SERVES 4

1.4kg (3lb) free-range chicken, jointed
175g (6oz) tamarind pulp
500ml (16fl oz) boiling water
Half-a-dozen cloves garlic, very finely chopped
4–6 shallots, very finely chopped
175g (6oz) palm or demerara sugar
60ml (2fl oz) dark soy sauce
A good handful of toasted coriander seeds, ground
Salt
Freshly ground black pepper

Wash the chicken well and pat dry with kitchen paper. Put the tamarind pulp into a bowl and add the boiling water. Mash it thoroughly and then strain into a large bowl. Throw in the garlic, shallots, sugar and soy sauce.

Add the chicken to the tamarind marinade, rolling it over several times. Cover and leave in a cool place to marinate overnight or at least for 4 hours.

Put the chicken and marinade in a flameproof casserole. Sprinkle over the coriander. Bring to the boil on top of the stove. Cover and simmer away for about 40 minutes, or until the chicken is tender and the liquid has reduced. This is quite a dry dish – most of the sauce should be absorbed by the chicken pieces. Season to taste with salt and pepper. Serve with some coconut rice and a pineapple and coconut sambal.

ROAST CHICKEN
Thailand

While we were filming at my chum Chom's country retreat, two elderly ladies were sitting cross-legged on the floor grinding fresh herbs in a pestle and mortar and fiddling with a couple of chickens as well as a large square empty oil container with the top taken off. After they had marinated and stuffed the chickens, they hung them inside the tin and placed the tin on a metal tray.

To my astonishment, they took it outside on to a track that ran through the paddy fields, and covered the tin with a small mountain of dried hay. It was a mound about three feet high and four to five feet in diameter.

My chum Chom said, 'We will now roast a chicken in eight minutes.' So saying, she set fire to the hay, which blazed furiously for about eight or ten minutes, until the blackened tin stood exposed in a circle of very fine ash. Chom gingerly lifted up the tin, unhooked the chickens from the wire and placed two succulent roast chickens on to a banana palm. As one we rushed at them and, using our hands, demolished the lot in seconds flat. If you don't have any hay, I'm afraid you will have to cook it in the oven.

SERVES 4

1.4–1.6kg (3–3½lb) free-
range chicken
4 cloves garlic
2 fresh coriander roots
Black peppercorns
Salt
1 tablespoon light soy sauce
2 blades of lemon grass,
crushed

A few pandan leaves or a
vanilla pod
A few galangal leaves, if
possible, or use Kaffir lime
leaves
A little coconut milk

Give the chicken a good rinse under running water and pat it dry with kitchen paper.

Using a pestle and mortar or a small blender, pound or mix together the garlic, coriander roots, peppercorns, salt and soy sauce.

Rub the marinade thoroughly into the skin of the chicken and also inside. Stuff the chicken with the lemon grass, *pandan* or vanilla pod, and galangal or lime leaves. Brush lightly with coconut milk and roast in a preheated oven, 200°C/400°F (gas mark 6), for 15–20 minutes per 450g (1lb), until it is tender. When the thigh is pierced with the point of a sharp knife, the juices should run clear and not be tinged with pink at all.

CHICKEN WITH LEMON GRASS
Vietnam

This is a refreshing, tangy dish. Just one word of warning: take care
not to burn the sugar.

SERVES 4

*900g (2lb) free-range chicken
breast fillets, skinned and
cubed
2 tablespoons fish sauce
2 teaspoons finely chopped
garlic
3 tablespoons white sugar*

*1 blade of lemon grass, finely
chopped
1 teaspoon freshly ground
black pepper
2 tablespoons groundnut oil
Slivers of seeded red chilli
pepper*

Marinate the chicken in the fish sauce, garlic, 1 tablespoon sugar, the
lemon grass and pepper for 30 minutes.

Heat the oil in a large, lidded pan and sauté the chicken until it is
golden. Lower the heat, cover and simmer until the chicken is tender,
about 20 minutes.

Meanwhile, caramelise the rest of the sugar by heating it over a
medium heat in a very small pan. Don't take your eyes off it as it turns
liquid and bubbly. As soon as it becomes golden brown, take it off the
heat. Immediately stir in the slivers of chilli and mix them into the
chicken, heat through and serve with steamed rice.

VIETNAMESE FRIED CHICKEN
Vietnam

SERVES 3–4

2 tablespoons light soy sauce
2 tablespoons fish sauce
Freshly ground black pepper
2 teaspoons brown sugar
5 cloves garlic, crushed and
  ground to a paste

4 shallots, thinly sliced
900g (2lb) free-range chicken,
  cut into 8 pieces
A little plain flour for coating
Groundnut oil for deep-frying

Mix together the soy and fish sauces. Add black pepper to taste. Stir in the sugar, garlic and shallots. No salt is needed as the fish sauce is salty enough.

Rub the mixture all over the chicken pieces and leave in a cool place to marinate for at least an hour.

Remove the chicken and sprinkle the pieces with a little flour. Heat about 5cm (2 inches) oil in a deep-fryer or wok, and deep-fry the chicken pieces a few at a time, until tender and golden with lovely crispy skins – about 8–10 minutes.

Remove the pieces as they are cooked, drain on kitchen paper and keep warm. Serve with boiled rice and your favourite dipping sauce.

STIR-FRIED CHICKEN WITH GREEN CURRY PASTE AND BASIL
Thailand

This simple dish is an example of the cross-fertilisation between Thai and Chinese kitchens. We ate it at a simple street stall on Ko Samui. We so thoroughly enjoyed it and had such attentive service from some extremely beautiful Thai waitresses that, after we had paid the bill, we presented them with a large tip saying, as you would in England, 'This is for you'.

One girl became rather excited and said, 'You want me?' Slight confusion there, but we managed to dissuade her from packing her bags and coming with us. It was she who said to us before we left, 'In Thailand, one smile makes two.'

SERVES 4

3 tablespoons vegetable oil
3 tablespoons green curry
  paste
450g (1lb) boned free-range
  chicken, sliced thinly
60ml (2fl oz) coconut milk
3 tablespoons brown sugar

3 tablespoons fish sauce
3 tablespoons seeded and
  sliced mixed red and green
  chilli peppers
2 fistfuls of fresh basil leaves
3 tablespoons coconut cream

Heat the oil in a wok or large frying pan. Stir in the green curry paste. Throw in the chicken and stir-fry quickly over a high heat, stirring and tossing it in the oil and paste, for 2–3 minutes. Add the coconut milk, sugar, fish sauce and chilli peppers. Cook for 5 minutes, stirring well. Just before serving, toss in the basil leaves. Pop a spoonful of coconut cream on top of each serving. This is excellent with steamed rice.

BARBECUED CHICKEN
Thailand

My chum Somchai organised a wonderful river trip in Mae Hong Son. We were tootling contentedly around a wide sweeping bend, filming as we went, when we encountered a spectacular sight. A boy of about twelve was wading across the river, bareback on an elephant.

It was a most impressive sight, rather spoiled by two boats of Japanese tourists who were so busy filming us that they practically drove into the elephant and caused it to stampede. Luckily the boy knew what to do, and got the terrified animal safely to the shore.

After that commotion, we pulled into the bank and before you could say Rudyard Kipling, Somchai had a fire going and was spit roasting chickens for our lunch.

SERVES 4

150ml (¼ pint) whisky, or brandy or sherry
2 tablespoons light soy sauce
2 tablespoons coconut milk
1 tablespoon fish sauce
4 cloves garlic, chopped
1 tablespoon chopped fresh coriander – root or leaf
A little chopped fresh root ginger

Salt
Freshly ground black pepper
1.4kg (3lb) free-range chicken, split in half through the breastbone and backbone – or ask your butcher to do it for you
Sliced raw vegetables of your choice, to garnish

Mix together the whisky, soy sauce, coconut milk, fish sauce, garlic, coriander, ginger and seasoning. Rub this marinade all over the chicken and leave for 30 minutes.

Then drain and cook the chicken in a preheated oven, 180°C/350°F (gas mark 4), for 40 minutes, until tender. To give it a lovely crispy brown finish, whack it on a barbecue or under a preheated hot grill for around 10–15 minutes. Serve with raw vegetables.

STIR-FRIED CHICKEN
Hong Kong

For stir-fried dishes, it is important that you have a really strong heat source and a plain metal wok or frying pan. These dishes really don't work in a non-stick pan on a bedsitters' single electric ring.

SERVES 4

2 tablespoons groundnut oil
450g (1lb) free-range chicken
  breast fillet, skinned and
  sliced paper thin
4 cloves garlic, finely chopped
3 shallots, finely chopped
1 large red or green chilli
  pepper, seeded and thinly
  sliced

5cm (2 inch) piece fresh root
  ginger, finely chopped
Freshly ground black pepper,
  rice vinegar and dark soy
  sauce, to taste

Heat the oil in a wok or frying pan and cook the chicken quickly over a fierce heat for 1 minute, then remove and put on one side.

Sauté the garlic, shallots, chilli and ginger for 30 seconds. Pop the chicken back into the pan. Add pepper, vinegar and dark soy sauce to season. Stir together for about 30 seconds and serve.

BEEF
AND PORK

BEEF RENDANG
Malaysia

Beef or Chicken Rendang is one of Malaysia's classic dishes. It is dry and hot. I ate it every day for breakfast while I was staying in Malacca.

SERVES 8–10

4–8 dried red chilli peppers, seeded and finely chopped
4–6 shallots, finely chopped
1 tablespoon finely chopped garlic
1.4kg (3lb) brisket of beef or braising steak, cut into large chunks
Salt
Freshly ground black pepper

4 tablespoons groundnut oil
½ teaspoon tamarind concentrate
1 tablespoon ground turmeric
1 blade of lemon grass, halved lengthways
350ml (12fl oz) thick coconut milk
2–3 Kaffir lime leaves
1½ tablespoons lime juice

Right, first grind the chillies, shallots and garlic to form a paste in a blender or a pestle and mortar. Season the beef with salt and pepper. Heat the oil in a flameproof casserole and quickly brown the beef. Remove.

Fry the paste for a minute or two, taking care not to let it burn, then add all the remaining ingredients. Add the browned beef, cover and cook gently for about 1 hour, until the meat is tender. It is a fairly dry curry. Serve with pineapple and cucumber sambal and coconut rice.

BEEF OR CHICKEN SATAY WITH PEANUT SAUCE
Malaysia

These delightful little kebabs are available from street hawkers throughout south-east Asia, and make a terrific snack. They were introduced by the Arabs centuries ago.

SERVES 4–6

4 shallots, finely chopped
3 blades of lemon grass, finely chopped
2.5cm (1 inch) piece fresh root ginger, finely chopped
½ teaspoon ground aniseed
1 teaspoon ground cumin
1 teaspoon ground turmeric
3 teaspoons ground coriander

75g (3 oz) brown sugar
Salt
700g (1½lb) lean beef such as fillet, or boneless chicken breast, cut into bite-size pieces
3 tablespoons groundnut oil
3 tablespoons thick coconut milk

Using a blender or pestle and mortar, grind together the shallots, lemon grass and ginger. Pop into a bowl and add the ground spices, sugar and salt. Add the meat to the bowl and coat well in the thick marinade. Cover and leave in the fridge to marinate for a few hours.

Soak wooden satay sticks in water so they don't catch fire during cooking. Thread a few pieces of meat on to each skewer, leaving around 2.5cm (1 inch) at the pointed end of each stick without meat. Mix together the oil and coconut milk and use this to baste the meat during cooking.

Grill the satays over a barbecue or under a preheated hot grill for about 6–8 minutes, turning and basting during cooking. Serve with Peanut Sauce.

PEANUT SAUCE

8 shallots, chopped
1 blade of lemon grass,
  chopped
2.5cm (1 inch) piece of fresh
  root ginger, chopped
3 tablespoons groundnut oil
1 tablespoon finely chopped
  seeded red chilli peppers

450g (1lb) roasted peanuts,
  ground
7 tablespoons caster sugar
2 tablespoons tamarind juice
Salt
300ml (½ pint water)

Using a pestle and mortar or blender, grind the shallots, lemon grass and ginger. Heat the oil in a pan and fry the ground shallot mixture for a few minutes, stirring well. Add the remaining ingredients and simmer for a couple of minutes, until the sauce is thick.

The sauce will keep well for a few days in the fridge. When reheating the sauce you will have to add more water to thin to the desired consistency.

DYNAMITE DRUNKEN BEEF
Thailand
PHOTOGRAPH OPPOSITE PAGE 176

This is an awesomely hot creation of my chum Chom, which takes its name from the small, very hot chillies known as bird's-eye or dynamite chillies. (Nothing to do with Captain Birdseye, by the way!)

SERVES 4

2 cloves garlic
2.5cm (1 inch) piece of galangal, chopped
2 shallots, chopped
2 chilli peppers (preferably bird's-eye), seeded and chopped
2 tablespoons groundnut oil
700g (1½lb) lean beef, such as fillet, thinly sliced
A few fresh green peppercorns
1 red and 1 green chilli pepper, seeded and sliced lengthways

2–3 Kaffir lime leaves, torn
100g (4oz) green beans, cut into 2.5cm (1 inch) lengths
1 tablespoon fish sauce
1 teaspoon palm or demerara sugar
2 teaspoons white distilled vinegar or rice vinegar
Whisky, to flame
About 8 fresh holy basil leaves (ordinary sweet basil will do)

Using a pestle and mortar or small blender, pound or mix together the garlic, galangal, shallots and chillies.

Heat the oil in a wok or frying pan and fry the pounded garlic mixture for a few minutes. Add the beef, peppercorns, chillies, lime leaves and green beans. Stir-fry over a high heat for about 5 minutes. The vegetables should still be crisp and bright-coloured. Pop in the fish sauce, brown sugar and vinegar and mix well.

Pour in a generous tot of the whisky and set it alight to 'flame' the dish. Reduce the heat and stir in the basil leaves just before serving. Serve on a bed of steamed rice.

FRIED BEEF WITH CASHEW NUTS
Thailand
PHOTOGRAPH OPPOSITE PAGE 145

This is an example of Thais taking a basic Chinese dish and refining it
to suit their love of fiery food.

I cooked this on Ko Samui and was able to use the fresh cashew nuts
that are grown on the island. And their oily, nutty, crunchy texture goes
really well with the tender strips of beef.

SERVES 4

2 tablespoons groundnut or
  sesame oil
2.5cm (1 inch) piece of fresh
  root ginger, finely chopped
  or grated
1 onion, halved and sliced
1 clove garlic, finely chopped
450g (1lb) lean beef, such as
  fillet, thinly sliced and cut
  into strips
Ground white pepper
1 teaspoon brown sugar
2 tablespoons light soy sauce

1 small green and 1 small red
  pepper, seeded and thinly
  sliced lengthways
3 spring onions, sliced
  diagonally
2 stalks celery, chopped
About 6 pieces of dried
  Chinese black mushrooms,
  soaked, drained and
  chopped (optional)
4 tablespoons roasted cashew
  nuts
2–4 tablespoons beef stock
Celery leaves, to garnish

Heat the oil in a wok or frying pan. Add the ginger, onion and garlic
and stir-fry over a high heat for 2–3 minutes. Throw in the beef and
stir-fry for a further 2–3 minutes, until browned. Season to taste with
the pepper, sugar and soy sauce.

Add the green and red peppers, spring onions, celery, mushrooms
and nuts. Pour in a little beef stock and stir-fry for about 3 minutes.
Garnish with celery leaves, if you like. Serve with white rice noodles.

PORK AND PRAWN STEW
Vietnam

CENTRE-SPREAD PHOTOGRAPH BETWEEN PAGES 144 AND 145

I cooked this dish for a Vietnamese Army volleyball team on a portable stove at the edge of their pitch – while they were playing. I came close to losing the lot on occasions, as the odd errant ball bounced on to the table. Anyway, they devoured it all and scraped their bowls clean.

SERVES 4

450g (1lb) pork tenderloin, cut into 2.5cm (1 inch) pieces
2 cloves garlic, finely chopped or minced
3 shallots, finely chopped
3 tablespoons fish sauce
3 spring onions, finely chopped
2 tablespoons groundnut oil

4–6 tablespoons brown sugar
300ml (½ pint) coconut water (from two fresh coconuts)
225g (8oz) raw prawns, shelled and deveined
2 teaspoons finely chopped or minced fresh root ginger
2 red chilli peppers, seeded and sliced

Marinate the pork with half the garlic, the shallots, 2 tablespoons fish sauce and the spring onions for at least 30 minutes.

Heat half the oil in a pan and sprinkle in 2–3 tablespoons of sugar. Do not heat too quickly and watch it like a hawk. Just as the sugar begins to caramelise and turn a toffee colour, add the marinated pork and stir into the oil and sugar, coating well. This seals the meat and colours the sauce you are going to make. Cook until the pork has turned a deep golden brown (coloured by the sugar), then add the coconut water. Simmer gently until the stock is reduced and the meat tender, about 30 minutes.

Meanwhile, marinate the prawns in the remaining fish sauce, ginger and remaining garlic for 15 minutes. Fry the prawns in sugared oil (as for the pork), until they change colour. Add them to the stew shortly before the cooking is complete. Garnish with sliced chillies and serve with steamed rice.

PORK AND LEMON GRASS BALLS
Thailand

I cooked this over a little charcoal stove on the mud floor 'kitchen' of a bamboo hut. It belonged to the chief of a hill tribe on the Burmese border, in north-eastern Thailand. So you shouldn't have any trouble at all preparing this tasty dish in your kitchen at home.

SERVES 4

450g (1lb) lean minced pork
½ teaspoon salt
4 blades of lemon grass, finely chopped
2 tablespoons red curry paste
A few Kaffir lime leaves, finely shredded

1–2 tomatoes, skinned and chopped
1 teaspoon ground turmeric
1 teaspoon minced galangal
Groundnut or sunflower oil for frying

Put all the ingredients, except the oil, into a bowl and mix well together. Use your hands and shape into walnut-size balls. Deep-fry in about 2.5cm (1 inch) hot oil in a wok, a few at a time, for 4–5 minutes, until golden brown. Serve with steamed rice.

CURRIES

PINEAPPLE AND PRAWN CURRY
Malaysia

This very simple dish relies on good quality fresh prawns and a sweet, ripe fresh pineapple. And the coconut milk and the ground nuts give it a beautiful, nutty, creamy taste.

SERVES 3–4

1 small ripe pineapple
1 red and 1 green chilli pepper,
　seeded and chopped
12 shallots, chopped
Half-a-dozen Brazil or
　macadamia nuts
1 blade of lemon grass,
　chopped

1 tablespoon finely chopped
　fresh root ginger
3 tablespoons groundnut oil
　or ghee
300ml (½ pint) coconut milk
350g (12oz) cooked prawns,
　shelled and seasoned with
　salt
Fish sauce

Peel and core the pineapple, then cut the flesh into rough triangles. In a pestle and mortar or blender, grind together the chillies, shallots, nuts, lemon grass and ginger to make a seasoning paste.

Heat the oil or ghee in a wok or pan and fry the pounded mixture for a couple of minutes. Stir in the coconut milk. Bring to the boil, then add the pineapple and cook gently for about 5 minutes, until nearly tender. Add the prawns and a little fish sauce to taste. Heat through for a couple of minutes, then serve.

PINEAPPLE AND MUSSEL CURRY
Thailand

Another fruity, fishy, fiery creation from my chum Chom, a perfect dish
to have on a warm sunny Sunday morning on your lawn.

SERVES 2–3

1 pineapple
700g (1½lb) mussels in shells,
  cleaned, bearded and rinsed
7.5cm (3 inch) piece of
  galangal, sliced
2 blades of lemon grass,
  chopped and lightly crushed
10 fresh holy basil sprigs (or
  use ordinary sweet basil)
1 tablespoon groundnut oil

1 tablespoon red curry paste
4 tablespoons coconut cream
1 tablespoon fish sauce
1 teaspoon palm or demerara
  sugar
4 Kaffir lime leaves, torn into
  pieces
2 red chilli peppers, seeded
  and cut into thin strips
  lengthways

Cut the pineapple in half lengthways. Hollow out the pineapple halves,
reserving the 'shells'. Discard the pineapple core and chop the flesh
into small pieces.

Throw the mussels, galangal, lemon grass and basil into a large pan.
Add water to a depth of 1cm (½ inch). Cover the pan, bring to the
boil and cook for 5–10 minutes, shaking the pan frequently, until the
mussels have opened. Discard any that remain closed.

Arrange the cooked mussels in the pineapple shells.

Heat the oil in a pan or wok and cook the red curry paste for a minute
to release the aroma. Carefully stir in the coconut cream, fish sauce,
brown sugar, lime leaves and chillies. Add the chopped pineapple and
heat through for a minute or two. Pour over the mussels in the pineapple shells and serve.

COCONUT FISH CURRY
Malaysia

SERVES 3–4

3 medium sole, John Dory or
  flounder, skinned, filleted
  and cut into small pieces
500ml (16fl oz) thin coconut
  milk
Salt
2–3 tablespoons groundnut
  oil
1–2 shallots, sliced
2 tablespoons red chilli
  peppers, seeded and finely
  chopped

2 teaspoons fish paste
1 teaspoon ground turmeric
2 teaspoons grated fresh root
  ginger
2 teaspoons brown sugar
120ml (4fl oz) tamarind
  water, or lime juice
225ml (8fl oz) thick coconut
  milk
Freshly ground black pepper

Put the fish, coconut milk and a little salt into a large pan. Cook gently for about 5 minutes until the fish is just cooked. Remove from the heat and put aside.

Heat the oil in a frying pan and sauté the shallots for about 5 minutes, until they are brown and crisp. Add the chillies and cook for a minute. Stir in the fish paste, turmeric and ginger to make your seasoning mix. Cook for a couple of minutes before adding the sugar and tamarind water or lime juice, and then simmer for 5 minutes.

Stir in the thick coconut milk and season with salt and pepper to taste. Drain the fish, discarding the liquid, and add to the pan. Heat through for a minute and serve.

STEAMED FISH CURRY WITH HERBS
Thailand

This is a splendid curry which I cooked in my chum Chom's house, which is a beautiful hardwood bungalow set on stilts at the edge of a rice paddy field some twenty miles east of Bangkok.

The great advantage of steaming is that it is a gentle process and it doesn't overcook or damage the fish. I commend it to the house!

SERVES 4

Spinach or blanched cabbage
   leaves
1–2 sprigs basil leaves
1–2 sprigs mint leaves
2 eggs, beaten
300ml (10fl oz) coconut cream
2 tablespoons fish sauce
3 tablespoons red curry paste

450g (1lb) bass (or other firm
   white fish), sliced thinly
4 Kaffir lime leaves, shredded
1 red and 1 green chilli pepper,
   seeded and finely sliced
1 tablespoon roughly chopped
   fresh coriander

Use a deep dish that will fit in a steamer. Line the dish with either spinach or blanched cabbage leaves and the basil and mint leaves.

Mix together the eggs, coconut cream, fish sauce and red curry paste and stir well.

Fold in the fish and pour this mixture into the lined dish. Sprinkle the lime leaves, chillies and coriander on top. Cover with foil or a heatproof plate. Steam for 15–20 minutes from the time the steamer water has started to boil. Serve from the bowl with rice.

CHICKEN CURRY WITH COCONUT CREAM AND SWEET POTATOES
Vietnam

CENTRE-SPREAD PHOTOGRAPH BETWEEN PAGES 112 AND 113

I had great fun cooking this mild and slightly sweet curry on the roof of a boat, drifting up and down the river in Saigon. It seems completely mad to cook things on the roof of a boat when you can do it in a perfectly good kitchen, but that's what filming is all about.

SERVES 4

2 tablespoons groundnut oil
1 onion, minced or grated
1 teaspoon minced garlic
1 blade of lemon grass, finely chopped
2 teaspoons mild curry powder
1 teaspoon ground turmeric
2 teaspoons crushed dried red chilli peppers
450g (1lb) skinned free-range chicken breast fillets, cubed

About 150ml (¼ pint) chicken stock
225ml (8fl oz) coconut cream
450g (1lb) sweet potato (or pumpkin), cubed and deep-fried
Salt
Freshly ground black pepper
1 teaspoon sugar
Red chilli peppers, seeded and sliced, to garnish

Heat the oil in a large pan or wok and cook the onion and garlic until softened. Add the lemon grass, curry powder, turmeric and dried red chillies. Cook for 2–3 minutes. Add the chicken pieces and coat well with the spices. Pour in enough chicken stock to cover, then simmer until the stock has well reduced. Add the coconut cream and cook for about 20 minutes, until the chicken is tender. If you are using a wok, cook over a low heat and keep an eye on it, stirring from time to time. Add the cubes of potato (or pumpkin) approximately 10 minutes before the end of the cooking time. Season with salt, pepper and sugar.

Garnish with slices of fresh red chillies and serve with warm crispy bread or a side dish of stir-fried matchstick courgettes sprinkled with sesame seeds.

CHICKEN CURRY
Malaysia

A simple, Indian-influenced creamy curry for those who find the Chicken or Beef Rendang too fierce.

SERVES 4

450g (1lb) boned free-range chicken meat, cut into bite-size pieces
3 teaspoons chilli powder
2 tablespoons groundnut oil or ghee
6 shallots, finely chopped
3 cloves garlic, finely chopped
3 red chilli peppers, seeded and finely chopped

2.5cm (1 inch) piece of fresh root ginger, finely chopped
A few curry leaves
A couple of bay leaves
1 blade of lemon grass, chopped
2 teaspoons ground cumin
300ml (10fl oz) thick coconut milk
Salt

Sprinkle the chicken with the chilli powder. Heat the oil or ghee in a frying pan or wok that has a lid and brown the chicken pieces. Lift out and keep warm. Pop in the shallots and garlic to the pan and stir-fry for a couple of minutes. Add all the remaining ingredients. Stir in the chicken. Bring to the boil. Cover and simmer for about 30 minutes, until the chicken is tender and the sauce thick. Don't forget to fish out the bay and curry leaves before serving.

CHICKEN AND BAMBOO SHOOT CURRY
Thailand

Fresh bamboo shoots are nutty and crunchy and contrast well with the tender chicken. If ever you find yourself in Mae Hong Son, make a beeline for Fern's Restaurant and try one there. It's brilliant.

SERVES 4

2 tablespoons groundnut oil
1 tablespoon red curry paste
6 tablespoons coconut cream
225g (8oz) can bamboo shoots, drained and cut into small pieces
5 Kaffir lime leaves, chopped
½ teaspoon brown sugar
2 teaspoons fish sauce

4 boneless free-range chicken breasts, cooked, skinned and cut into small strips – ideally, the chicken should be poached so that it is not too dry
2 red chilli peppers, seeded and sliced
2 teaspoons chopped fresh basil
1 teaspoon chopped fresh mint

Heat the oil in a large wok or frying pan. Stir in the red curry paste and cook for a minute to release the flavours. Add the coconut cream carefully so the pan doesn't sizzle or spit. Throw in the bamboo shoots, lime leaves, sugar and fish sauce. Mix well together.

Pop in the chicken pieces and heat through thoroughly for about 5 minutes. Just before serving, stir in the chillies, chopped basil and mint.

MALAYSIAN BEEF CURRY
Malaysia

SERVES 4

A chunk of ghee or 2
   tablespoons groundnut oil
1 teaspoon ground cinnamon
1 teaspoon ground cumin
1 teaspoon chopped star anise
2 whole cardamoms, crushed
4 whole cloves
2 curry or bay leaves
1 tablespoon grated fresh root
   ginger
6 shallots, chopped

450g (1lb) lean stewing steak,
   cubed
2 tablespoons mild curry
   powder
3 medium potatoes, peeled and
   cubed
3 green chilli peppers, seeded
   and finely chopped
425ml (¾ pint) coconut milk
Salt
Juice of 1 lime

Heat the ghee or oil in a large pan and sauté the cinnamon, cumin, star anise, cardamoms, cloves and curry or bay leaves for a minute. Stir in the ginger and shallots and cook for another couple of minutes. Pop in the meat and cook until browned.

Stir in the curry powder, potatoes and chillies. Add the coconut milk. Cover and simmer for about 45 minutes, or until the meat is tender. Stir well and often during cooking. Season with salt and add lime juice to taste just before serving. Fish out the bay or curry leaves.

CHIANG MAI CURRY
Thailand

This is a catch-all, one-pot fiery curry, often described in translation as 'jungle curry'. It is runny and spicy but it may contain, up in those remote areas, some culinary surprises. My recipe uses beef, but in that part of the world snake, frog, wild boar, assorted birds and unspecified furry creatures would often be used. You could, though, substitute the beef for tenderloin or fillet of pork.

SERVES 4

2 tablespoons yellow bean sauce
2 tablespoons red curry paste
4 green chilli peppers, seeded and chopped
2 tablespoons caster sugar
4 cloves garlic, chopped
3 shallots, chopped
1 tablespoon chopped lemon grass
1 tablespoon chopped fresh root ginger
Dash of shrimp paste
60ml (2fl oz) tamarind water – or use lime juice
450g (1lb) braising steak (shin of beef etc), thinly sliced, then cut into strips
500ml (16fl oz) coconut milk

Using a pestle and mortar or blender, mix the yellow bean sauce, red curry paste, chillies, sugar, garlic, shallots, lemon grass, ginger, shrimp paste and tamarind or lime juice to a paste.

Put the beef and coconut milk into a flameproof casserole. Bring to the boil. Cover and simmer gently for about 45 minutes, or until the meat is tender. Add the blended ingredients and mix thoroughly. Cover and cook for a further 10 minutes.

GREEN BEEF CURRY
Thailand

SERVES 3–4

2 tablespoons groundnut oil
3 tablespoons green chilli
    paste (see below)
350g (12oz) fillet of beef,
    thinly sliced and then cut
    into strips
425ml (15fl oz) coconut cream
2 tablespoons fish sauce
1 tablespoon brown sugar

1 aubergine, peeled, cubed and
    blanched
A few fresh green peppercorns
1 red and 1 green chilli pepper,
    seeded and finely chopped
2.5cm (1 inch) fresh root
    ginger, chopped
3–4 Kaffir lime leaves, torn
    into pieces
Fresh basil leaves

Heat the oil in a large pan and add the chilli paste. Cook for a minute. Add the beef and stir-fry over a high heat for a minute.

Add the coconut cream, fish sauce and sugar and bring to the boil. Cook for a minute, stirring them round the pan.

Add the aubergine, peppercorns, chillies, ginger and lime leaves. Cook for about 2 minutes, sprinkle with the basil leaves and serve.

CHILLI PASTE

1 teaspoon cumin seeds,
    roasted and ground
1 teaspoon coriander seeds,
    roasted and ground
1 teaspoon shrimp paste
1 green chilli pepper, seeded
    and chopped
2–4 bird's-eye chilli peppers,
    seeded and chopped
grated zest of 1 lime
    (preferably Kaffir)

1 blade of lemon grass,
    chopped
2 cloves garlic, chopped
2–3 shallots, chopped
Salt
2.5cm (1 inch) piece of
    galangal, chopped
2.5cm (1 inch) piece of fresh
    root ginger, chopped

Using a pestle and mortar, blender or food processor, grind together all the ingredients to make a smooth paste.

PORK CURRY
Burma

Before I went to north-west Thailand, the culinary European gurus that I met in Bangkok claimed that the food up there was strongly influenced by Burma. I found no evidence at all to support this theory and even Somchai, who is a brilliant chef, couldn't explain to me what was Burmese about this particular dish.

Personally I don't care where it comes from, it tastes great.

SERVES 4

2 tablespoons groundnut oil or ghee
2 cloves garlic, finely chopped
4 shallots, finely chopped
700g (1½lb) lean pork shoulder or tenderloin, cut into 2.5cm (1 inch) pieces
2 tablespoons chopped fresh root ginger
1 teaspoon ground turmeric
½ teaspoon palm or demerara sugar
1 teaspoon mild curry powder
Approx. 4–6 tablespoons vegetable stock
1 tablespoon light soy sauce
2 tablespoons grated fresh coconut
50g (2oz) roasted peanuts, chopped

Heat the oil or ghee in a large pan. Add the garlic, shallots, pork and ginger and fry briskly until browned. Lower the heat and stir in the turmeric, sugar and curry powder. Cook for a few minutes. Add the stock, soy sauce and coconut and cook gently for about 30 minutes, or until the pork is tender. If the pork becomes too dry add a little more stock during cooking. Serve sprinkled with the chopped nuts.

RICE
AND NOODLES

FRIED RICE WITH BASIL AND PORK
Thailand

SERVES 4

3 tablespoons groundnut oil
175g (6oz) loin of pork, diced
  or thinly sliced
3 tablespoons seeded and
  finely chopped green chilli
  peppers
2 tablespoons finely chopped
  shallots
3 cloves garlic, finely chopped
¼ teaspoon white pepper

About 4 cups steamed long-
  grain rice
2 tablespoons brown sugar
1 tablespoon light soy sauce
90ml (3fl oz) fish sauce
5 tablespoons roughly
  chopped fresh basil leaves
Sliced cucumber, carrot,
  tomato – anything you like,
  to garnish

Heat the oil in a wok or large frying pan and add the pork, chillies, shallots, garlic and pepper, and stir-fry for 3–4 minutes. Add the rice, sugar, soy sauce and fish sauce. Stir well and stir-fry for about 3 minutes, or until the rice is heated through. Add the basil leaves, garnish and serve.

COCONUT RICE
Malaysia

Don't use rice that is old or too dry as it will need more
water to cook in.

SERVES 8

450g (1lb) long-grain rice | 1 teaspoon salt
725ml (1¼ pints) thin
   coconut milk

Wash the rice thoroughly until the water runs clear. Put the rice in a
heavy pan and add the coconut milk and salt. Bring to the boil, stirring.
Reduce the heat and simmer gently for 12 minutes, covered with a
tight-fitting lid. Remove from the heat and stand covered with the lid
for a further 10 minutes. It will finish cooking in its own steam. Fluff
up with a fork or chopsticks.

Opposite: Dynamite Drunken Beef (page 160)
Next page, clockwise from top: Grilled Lime-flavoured Mini Ribs
(page 195); Beef Meatballs with Lime (page 193) surrounded
by Crispy Pork in Mangetout (page 195); Asparagus Steamed with
Ginger and Lime (page 194); Honeyed Quail (page 191)

STICKY RICE WITH CHICKEN AND PORK
Malaysia

CENTRE-SPREAD PHOTOGRAPH BETWEEN PAGES 144 AND 145

SERVES 6

2½ tablespoons light soy
   sauce
2 tablespoons oyster sauce
1 tablespoon brown sugar
225g (8oz) free-range chicken
   breast fillets, skinned and
   cut into bite-size pieces
350g (12oz) lean pork, diced
Groundnut oil for frying
50g (2oz) shiitake
   mushrooms, sliced

1 tablespoon cornflour
   (optional)
450g (1lb) sticky rice
   (short or round grain)
   soaked in water overnight,
   then drained
Salt
Freshly ground black pepper
Chopped fresh coriander
   leaves

Put the soy sauce, oyster sauce and sugar into a bowl and mix together. Pop about three-quarters of this mixture into a large bowl and add the chicken and pork. Coat well in the mixture.

Heat a little oil in a wok or large frying pan and cook the chicken and pork for about 5 minutes until golden. Add the mushrooms and a little water. Cover and simmer for about 20 minutes, until the pork and chicken are tender. If the sauce is very thin, thicken it with the cornflour mixed with a little water.

Mix the drained rice with the remaining soy sauce mixture and seasoning.

Put some chicken and pork mixture into the bottom of individual heatproof bowls. Top up to the halfway mark with rice. Steam over boiling water for about 30 minutes, until the rice is cooked. You can either do this by putting the bowls into a bamboo steamer and setting this on a rack in a large wok or placing them in a normal steamer. Remember to keep the water topped up. Turn out and sprinkle with coriander leaves.

Top Vegetable Curry Salad (page 188); **Bottom** Duck Salad with
Hot and Sour Dressing (page 187)

CHICKEN AND COCONUT MILK LAKSA
Malaysia

To my mind, this magnificent dish is the Asian answer to the Mediterranean *bouillabaisse* and *bourride*. I know it looks a little complicated, but it is well worth the effort involved. The combination of ingredients is infinitely variable and you could, for instance, throw in a handful of shrimps if you had some, too. It's probably a good idea to read my notes on pages 36–7 before you begin to prepare your *Laksa*.

SERVES 4

3 tablespoons oil, preferably peanut
225g (8oz) pressed beancurd, cut into cubes
3 medium onions, peeled – one sliced finely and two diced finely
1 teaspoon finely chopped garlic
3 Brazil nuts, grated or finely chopped
2 teaspoons ground cumin
1 tablespoon ground coriander
1 tablespoon chopped green or red chilli peppers
½ teaspoon shrimp paste
1–2 tablespoons rempah, see page 128, or red curry paste

1 litre (1¾ pints) thin coconut milk
1 tablespoon brown sugar
Salt
Freshly ground black pepper
450g (1lb) cooked free-range chicken, skinned, boned and chopped
225g (8oz) beansprouts, blanched
225g (8oz) rice noodles, cooked

To garnish:
1 tablespoon chopped spring onions
Fresh coriander leaves
Fresh red chilli pepper, seeded and chopped

Heat 1 tablespoon of the oil in a large pan. Fry the beancurd until golden and crunchy on the outside. Remove and put to one side. Keep warm.

Cook the sliced onion for about 5 minutes until golden and crispy. Lift out and set aside. Now add a further tablespoon of oil to the pan and cook the chopped onions and garlic for 2–3 minutes. Pop in the nuts, cumin, coriander, chillies, shrimp paste, and *rempah* or curry paste. Stir well and cook over a medium heat for about 2 minutes. Add the coconut milk, sugar and seasonings. Bring to the boil, then simmer for 10 minutes.

Heat the remaining oil in a frying pan or wok and stir-fry the chicken for 3–4 minutes. Chuck in the beansprouts and stir-fry for 1–2 minutes. Remove and keep warm.

Divide the noodles between 4 deep bowls. Add some fried sliced onion to each one. Top with the chicken, beansprouts and beancurd. Pour over the hot sauce. Garnish with the spring onions, coriander and chilli.

RICE IN BANANA LEAVES WITH COCONUT SAMBAL
Malaysia

PHOTOGRAPH OPPOSITE PAGE 144

Most banana leaves come ready-prepared in Asian stores and have had their spines removed. Soften the leaves first by quickly blanching them. They will impart a delicate flavour to the rice, but you can't eat them.

SERVES 4

2 cups long-grain rice	*4 banana leaves*

Put a mound of rice on to four banana leaves. Wrap them into little parcels, but be sure to leave plenty of room for the rice to swell. Tie up carefully with strips of banana leaf.

Pop the packets into a bamboo steamer and cook over boiling water for about 2 hours. If you need to, add more water – in much the same way as you did with Christmas puddings before microwaves took over the earth.

The Malaysians call this *Lontong*, and it's scrumptious with a coconut sambal.

COCONUT SAMBAL

70g (2½oz) desiccated coconut	*2 shallots, chopped*
150ml (¼ pint) warm milk	*1 teaspoon paprika*
1 small red chilli pepper, seeded and chopped	*1 teaspoon lime juice*
	Salt

Soften the desiccated coconut in the milk for about 30 minutes. Squeeze out the liquid.

Put the chilli, shallots, paprika, lime juice and salt into a food processor and whizz until you have a paste. Mix the paste into the softened coconut. Use it as it is or, if you prefer, you can fry the mixture in a little groundnut oil.

YELLOW RICE
Malaysia

SERVES 8

450g (1lb) sticky rice (short or
   round grain)
7.5cm (3 inch) piece of fresh
   turmeric, cleaned and
   pounded and tied in muslin

12 white or black peppercorns
300ml (10fl oz) coconut milk,
   salted

Soak the rice overnight in water with the turmeric – this helps soften the grains. Rinse and drain.

To steam the rice, put in a steaming basket or use a nylon sieve set in a wooden band, over boiling water. Steam the rice with the peppercorns until cooked – about 25 minutes.

Mix together the rice and coconut milk and return to the steamer for a further 12 minutes. This is good with chicken or beef curry.

FRIED THAI NOODLES
Thailand

Tang Chi is sold whole or in slices in vacuum sealed packs in Chinese or Asian stores.

SERVES 2

4 tablespoons groundnut oil
2 shallots, thinly sliced
1 egg
100g (4oz) medium flat noodles, soaked in water for 20 minutes until soft, then drained
2 tablespoons lime or lemon juice
1 tablespoon fish sauce
½–1 teaspoon tamarind concentrate
1 teaspoon brown sugar
100g (4oz) beancurd, finely sliced and deep-fried

2 tablespoons roasted peanuts, chopped
2 tablespoons whole dried prawns, ground or pounded – rinse before use
1 tablespoon preserved radish (Tang Chi), finely chopped
25g (1oz) beansprouts
Chopped Chinese chives (or the green stalks of spring onion)
2 red chilli peppers, seeded and chopped
Sprigs of fresh coriander

In a wok or frying pan, heat the oil, add the shallots and fry for about 10 minutes, until tender and golden brown. Break the egg into the wok and stir quickly for a couple of seconds. Throw in the noodles and stir well. Mix well with the shallots and egg, scraping down the sides of the wok.

Add the lime or lemon juice, fish sauce, tamarind concentrate, sugar, beancurd, half the peanuts, half the dried prawns, the preserved radish, the beansprouts and chives. Stir-fry quickly for a couple of minutes. Serve sprinkled with the remaining peanuts, dried prawns and the chilli and coriander.

EGG FRIED NOODLES
Malaysia

SERVES 4

375g (12oz) egg noodles
Oil, peanut if possible
100g (4oz) chopped dark
  green leaves – use choy sum
225g (8oz) beansprouts
225g (8oz) cooked ham or
  bacon or pork, cut into strips
225g (8oz) small, raw prawns,
  shelled and deveined
1 cake of pressed beancurd or
  firm tofu, diced

2 teaspoons garlic, very finely
  chopped
2 tablespoons chilli paste
Salt
Freshly ground black pepper
Dark soy sauce
175ml (6fl oz) chicken stock
100g (4oz) spring onions,
  chopped

Plunge the noodles briefly into boiling water, and drain well.

Now you need to stir-fry all the main ingredients, one by one. Remove as each one is cooked and keep them all together. Start by heating some oil and quickly stir-frying the greens and beansprouts. Next, add the ham, bacon or pork and prawns (cook until the prawns turn pink), followed by the beancurd (which will probably need a little more oil).

Reheat the pan, add more oil as necessary, and fry the noodles on one side, then the other. Now it's the turn of the garlic and chilli paste. Tip back all the waiting ingredients and season with salt and pepper and soy sauce.

Pour in the chicken stock, bring up to the boil and stir in the spring onions. Cover and simmer until the noodles have absorbed the liquid, then serve.

VIETNAMESE CREPES
Vietnam

MAKES 8 CREPES

This lacy crepe, made with a flour and water batter, was the last in a long line of wonderful dishes cooked at Madame Dai's restaurant in Saigon. You could vary the filling as you wish – strips of cooked chicken and quickly stir-fried vegetables would be good.

100g (4oz) rice flour
Pinch of powdered saffron
About 150ml (¼ pint) water
1 egg, size 2
Vegetable oil for frying

For the filling:
Cooked and shelled prawns
Blanched beansprouts
Pork fat, cut into tiny dice and
 fried until browned
To serve, fish sauce or a
 dipping sauce as Nuoc
 Cham, *see page 197*

Put the rice flour, saffron, water and egg into a bowl and whisk well together. Use a well seasoned or non-stick, 18–20cm (7–8inch) pancake or omelette pan. Heat for 2–3 minutes. Put the batter into a jug. Brush the hot pan with a little vegetable oil. Hold the jug in one hand and the hot pancake pan in the other hand. Pour the batter from the jug in a thin, circular stream, at the same time tipping and swirling the pan so the batter thinly covers the surface. As the batter hits the pan it will 'splatter', giving a lacy effect. When the top of the pancake is set, loosen it and flip it over with a broad palette knife.

The pancakes should be thin and lacy. If the pancakes are too thick, then thin down the batter, with a couple of tablespoons of water; the batter should be very thin and watery. It is a good idea to stir the batter well between making each pancake. With a little practice (and a very hot pan), you should get 8 crepes out of this mixture.

Fill the pancakes with a mixture of prawns, beansprouts and pork fat. Fold each pancake in half and serve at once, while the pancake is still hot and crisp, with fish sauce or *Nuoc Cham*.

SALADS AND VEGETABLES

PAPAYA POK POK
Thailand

My chum Chom cooked this dish on the banks of the river in Mae Hong Son. This is typical street-style food, extremely popular in Bangkok where people buy it from street stalls. It is literally fresh papaya crushed in a pestle and mortar, with the other ingredients thrown in – a hot, spicy salad.

SERVES 2–3

3–4 cloves garlic, roughly chopped
2–3 bird's-eye chilli peppers, seeded and chopped
1 tablespoon dried salted shrimps, rinse before use
450g (1lb) green papaya, grated
4 tablespoons lime juice

2 tablespoons fish sauce
1 tablespoon brown sugar
1 tablespoon roasted peanuts, chopped
2 tomatoes, quartered
100g (4oz) cooked green beans, cut into 5cm (2 inch) lengths

Crush the garlic, chillies and dried shrimps with a pestle and mortar or a blender. Next, pop in the papaya and blend well. If you are making it in a blender, whizz only briefly so it is a slightly mashed consistency. Add the lime juice, fish sauce, brown sugar, peanuts, tomatoes and beans and mix well.

LOTUS SPROUT SALAD
Vietnam

Lotus sprouts are a cross between salsify and asparagus. They are not easy to find here, but I include the recipe just in case you do come across them as they are delicious.

SERVES 4

450g (1lb) lotus sprouts, peeled and cut into 7.5cm (3 inch) pieces
4 tablespoons white vinegar
225g (8oz) cooked prawns, shelled
225g (8oz) free-range cooked chicken breast fillet, shredded
2 carrots, grated
½ large cucumber, peeled, seeds removed, grated

1 tablespoon finely chopped fresh mint leaves
1 tablespoon finely chopped fresh coriander leaves
4 red chilli peppers, seeded and cut into flowers, fresh coriander leaves and finely sliced spring onion, to garnish

Marinate the lotus sprouts in the vinegar for 30 minutes. Drain well. Put in a bowl together with the prawns, chicken, carrots, cucumber and herbs and mix well. Fill small rice bowls with the mixture and press firmly down, then turn out on to a serving plate.

Garnish with a chilli 'flower', coriander leaves and spring onion slices.

Chilli flowers

To make these for a garnish, you need some firm chilli peppers. Using a sharp knife or small scissors, cut off the tip of each chilli. Carefully cut the chilli from tip to stem, but without cutting through the stem, four times at equal intervals. Remove the seeds. Then cut through each petal once or twice more to make finer petals. Put the chilli in a bowl of chilled water and pop in the fridge for 10–15 minutes. The petals will open up and curl back to look like a flower.

THAI CHICKEN SALAD
Thailand

SERVES 2

225g (8oz) cooked chicken,
  minced
4 tablespoons lime juice
2 tablespoons fish sauce
1 shallot, thinly sliced
2 teaspoons chopped fresh
  coriander

2 spring onions, chopped
Powdered dried chilli peppers
  and powdered roasted rice –
  grind in a food processor
A few fresh mint leaves

Mix together the chicken, lime juice and fish sauce. Then add the shallot, coriander and spring onions. Sprinkle the powdered chilli and rice into the mixture and stir again. Serve topped with mint leaves.

DUCK SALAD WITH HOT AND SOUR DRESSING
Thailand

PHOTOGRAPH OPPOSITE PAGE 177

SERVES 4

4 duck breast fillets, roasted or
  grilled and thinly sliced
Fresh crisp lettuce leaves
2 shallots, thinly sliced
4 spring onions, finely
  chopped
Matchstick batons of
  cucumber and celery
3 tablespoons fish sauce
1–2 tablespoons lime juice

2 cloves garlic, crushed or
  finely chopped
1 red and 1 green chilli pepper,
  seeded and very finely
  chopped
1 teaspoon palm or demerara
  sugar
Celery leaves, sliced seeded
  chilli pepper, chopped
  spring onions, to garnish

Arrange the slices of duck on a bed of lettuce on a serving dish. Sprinkle over the shallots, spring onions, cucumber and celery.

To make the dressing, put the fish sauce, lime juice, garlic, chillies and sugar into a small pan, and heat through gently. The actual amount of ingredients is just a guide and you can experiment with it until it is to your liking. Pour the warm dressing over the salad and garnish with the celery leaves, sliced chilli and chopped spring onions.

VEGETABLE CURRY SALAD
Thailand

PHOTOGRAPH OPPOSITE PAGE 177

SERVES 4–6

4 carrots, sliced
100g (4oz) white cabbage,
  sliced
225g (8oz) baby sweetcorn
225g (8oz) asparagus tips
100g (4oz) green beans, cut
  into 2.5cm (1 inch) pieces
1 aubergine, peeled and cut
  into dice
225g (8oz) beansprouts, well
  rinsed
100g (4oz) button
  mushrooms, sliced

For the sweet and sour
  curry sauce:
2 tablespoons coconut oil
1 tablespoon red curry paste

2 tablespoons coconut cream
1 tablespoon light soy sauce
1 teaspoon brown sugar
1 tablespoon tamarind water
Salt
1 teaspoon ground coriander
1 teaspoon ground cumin
2 tablespoons roasted peanuts,
  finely chopped

For the garnish:
3 shallots, sliced and deep-
  fried until golden
3–4 cloves garlic, sliced and
  deep-fried until golden
1 tablespoon toasted sesame
  seeds

Blanch the carrots, cabbage, sweetcorn, asparagus, green beans and aubergine in boiling water. Drain. Arrange the blanched vegetables in a salad bowl, together with the beansprouts and mushrooms.

Heat the oil in a pan and add the red curry paste. Stir for a minute to release the flavours. Carefully stir in the coconut cream, soy sauce, sugar, tamarind water, salt, coriander, cumin and peanuts. Pour over the vegetables.

Sprinkle with the deep-fried shallots, garlic and the toasted sesame seeds.

FRIED GREEN BEANS WITH PRAWNS
Thailand

SERVES 4

2 tablespoons vegetable oil
2 cloves garlic, crushed or
   minced
3 shallots, finely chopped or
   minced
1–2 red or green chilli peppers,
   seeded and chopped

1 teaspoon shrimp paste
450g (1lb) cooked prawns,
   shelled and chopped
225g (8oz) green beans, sliced
1 tablespoon fish sauce
2 teaspoons brown sugar

Heat the oil in a wok or frying pan. Stir-fry the garlic, shallots, chillies and shrimp paste over a high heat for half a minute. Throw in the prawns and green beans and stir-fry for about 5 minutes.

Season with fish sauce and sugar and serve hot with steamed rice.

STIR-FRYING Stir-frying is a very rapid process that requires your constant attention. For successful stir-frying the ingredients should be cut into small, even pieces, so that they cook quickly in the same amount of time. Meat should be sliced thinly and cut into strips. Place the wok over a high heat and add the oil. Heat the oil until almost smoking; this will happen very quickly in a wok. Add the ingredients and toss the food constantly, keeping it moving from the centre of the wok to the sides. Because the heat is kept high the cooking is very fast and vegetables especially should not be overcooked – they should remain crisp and bright coloured.

Electric or non-stick woks should be avoided as they don't reach sufficiently high temperatures.

BEANSPROUTS, STIR-FRIED WITH SHREDDED PORK
Hong Kong

SERVES 2–3

2 teaspoons light soy sauce
1 egg white, beaten
3 teaspoons cornflour
225g (8oz) lean pork, such as
  tenderloin, thinly sliced
  and cut in strips
225g (8oz) beansprouts
3 tablespoons groundnut oil

½ teaspoon finely chopped
  fresh root ginger
2 teaspoons finely chopped
  spring onions
1 tablespoon oyster sauce
1 teaspoon sugar
A few drops of sesame oil
90ml (3fl oz) chicken stock

Mix together the soy sauce, egg white and 2 teaspoons cornflour. Put this mixture into a bowl with the pork. Stir well and leave for 20 minutes.

Heat a wok or frying pan and dry stir-fry the beansprouts over a high heat for 1 minute. Remove. Heat the oil in the wok and stir-fry the pork for 1–2 minutes. Add the ginger, spring onions and beansprouts. Stir-fry briefly. Pop in the oyster sauce, sugar and sesame oil. Mix the chicken stock with the remaining 1 teaspoon cornflour. Add to the pan and stir until thickened.

STIR-FRIED SPINACH WITH GARLIC
Vietnam

PHOTOGRAPH OPPOSITE PAGE 113

SERVES 4

900g (2lb) spinach,
  thoroughly washed and
  trimmed
2 tablespoons peanut oil
6 cloves garlic, finely chopped

1 tablespoon fish sauce
Knob of butter
Freshly ground black pepper

Gently dry the spinach in a salad spinner or in a clean tea towel. Heat the oil in a large wok or frying pan, add the garlic and stir-fry for 1–2 minutes, until golden. Add the spinach and cook for 2–3 minutes. Stir in the fish sauce and the butter and liberally twist over some pepper.

PARTY FOOD

I have included the following eight recipes as an idea for a Chinese-style finger buffet when you have to entertain a dozen or so friends.

HONEYED QUAIL

CENTRE-SPREAD PHOTOGRAPH BETWEEN PAGES 176 AND 177

2 teaspoons clear honey
A little very hot water
2 teaspoons white wine
  vinegar
6 small quails, ready prepared,
  halved and wiped with
  kitchen towel

Salt
Groundnut or sunflower oil
  for deep-frying

Mix together the honey, water and wine vinegar and brush over the quails. Leave to dry for around 12 hours in a cool, well-ventilated place. Season the quails with a little salt.

Heat about 5cm (2 inches) oil in a large wok or deep frying pan and deep-fry the quail, two or three halves at a time, until they are tender and their skins are wonderfully crisp. This will take about 5 minutes, depending on their size. Serve warm.

CHICKEN AND CRAB ROLLS
Vietnam

For the filling:
225g (8oz) free-range chicken
   breast fillet, skinned and
   very finely chopped or
   minced
100g (4oz) cooked white
   crabmeat, flaked
50g (2oz) chopped, cooked rice
   vermicelli
About 10 spring onions,
   finely chopped
1 carrot, grated
1 egg, beaten
Salt
Freshly ground black pepper

Rice paper wrappers, each
   15cm (6 inches) in diameter
3 tablespoons light corn syrup
   (buy from delicatessens) or
   a little beaten egg
Groundnut oil for deep-frying

To serve:
Lettuce leaves
Fresh coriander leaves
Fresh basil leaves
Fish sauce or a dipping sauce
   such as Nuoc Cham – see
   page 197

Put the chicken, crabmeat, rice vermicelli, spring onions and carrot into a bowl. Add the egg and seasoning to taste and mix well together.

Dip the wrappers one at a time into cold water – this will soften them – and dry well with a kitchen towel. Brush one side of each wrapper with the syrup or some beaten egg and put a spoonful of the filling in the centre. Fold the edge nearest you to the middle. Fold both sides into the centre and roll up, sealing the last edge with a little water. Deep-fry the rolls in about 5cm (2 inches) hot oil, until they are cooked through, golden and crisp – about 5 minutes. Turn the rolls during cooking to ensure even browning.

To serve, wrap each roll in a lettuce leaf with a few coriander and basil leaves. Dip into fish sauce or Nuoc Cham and munch.

PS You can vary the fillings, of course. Pork and shrimp is very good – or for vegetarians, beancurd (tofu) and mushrooms.

BEEF MEATBALLS WITH LIME

CENTRE-SPREAD PHOTOGRAPH BETWEEN PAGES 176 AND 177

1 tablespoon dark soy sauce
2 teaspoons dry sherry
Couple of pinches of soft
 brown sugar
Couple of dashes of ginger
 wine
2 teaspoons cornflour
Zest and juice of ½ lime
4 tablespoons water
3 cloves garlic, very finely
 chopped

10 canned water chestnuts,
 drained and finely chopped
1–2 teaspoons sesame oil
450g (1lb) rump or fillet
 steak – very well minced
100ml (3½fl oz) vegetable oil
2 large cloves garlic, very
 lightly crushed

Mix together the soy sauce, sherry, sugar, ginger wine, cornflour, lime zest and juice. Stir in the water and mix well. Pop in the garlic, water chestnuts and sesame oil. Mix well together. Stir in the minced beef.

Take a small amount of mixture at a time and, using your hands, roll into walnut-sized balls.

Heat the oil with the garlic in a wok or frying pan. When the oil is hot remove the garlic and cook the meatballs in batches for 3–5 minutes. Roll them over during cooking so they are evenly browned. Serve hot with a choice of dipping sauces.

MINTY LAMB BALLS

350g (12oz) lean lamb,
   roughly chopped
50g (2oz) pork dripping
1 tablespoon light soy sauce
1 teaspoon soft brown sugar
3 shallots, finely chopped
Good fistful of fresh mint
   leaves, finely chopped
1 egg white
1 teaspoon cornflour
Plain flour

For the glaze:
2 teaspoons light soy sauce
2 teaspoons dry sherry
2 teaspoons groundnut oil
1 teaspoon sweet chilli sauce
1 teaspoon hoisin sauce

Groundnut or sunflower oil
   for deep-frying

Put the lamb into a food processor and whizz until minced. Add the dripping and whizz again. Pop in the soy sauce, sugar, shallots, mint, egg white and cornflour and blend briefly until well mixed.

With lightly floured hands, divide and shape into walnut-sized balls. Toss them in a little flour to coat. Put the glaze ingredients into a small saucepan and bring to the boil, stirring well. Remove from heat.

Heat the oil in a wok or deep frying pan and fry the meatballs a few at a time for about 3–5 minutes, or until golden brown. Drain well and roll in the glaze. Serve warm.

ASPARAGUS STEAMED WITH GINGER AND LIME

CENTRE-SPREAD PHOTOGRAPH BETWEEN PAGES 176 AND 177

1 tablespoon finely grated
   fresh root ginger
2 tablespoons lime juice
Salt
White pepper

3 tablespoons oil (a mix of
   sesame and corn is perfect)
1kg (2lb) fresh young
   asparagus tips

Make a dressing by whisking together the ginger, lime juice, salt and white pepper, then dribbling in the oil. Leave on one side.

Steam the asparagus until it is just tender. Let it cool a little and then serve with the dressing.

GRILLED LIME-FLAVOURED MINI RIBS

CENTRE-SPREAD PHOTOGRAPH BETWEEN PAGES 176 AND 177

700g (1½lb) spare ribs, either
   mini ribs or large ones
   chopped in half
Salt
Freshly ground black pepper
Juice and zest of 2 limes
60ml (2fl oz) malt vinegar

1 teaspoon dark soy sauce
2 tablespoons soft brown
   sugar
1 egg, beaten
Plain flour
Thin wedges of fresh lime, to
   garnish

Pop the spare ribs into a shallow dish and season well. Put the juice and zest of limes, vinegar, soy sauce and sugar into a bowl and mix thoroughly. Pour over the spare ribs. Cover and leave in a cool place for several hours. Turn the ribs in the marinade from time to time. Dip the spare ribs into the egg and then in flour. Shake off the excess flour.

Cook under a preheated medium grill for about 20 minutes, until tender and very dark brown in colour. Baste frequently with the marinade and turn over several times during cooking. Serve hot, garnished with thin wedges of lime.

CRISPY PORK IN MANGETOUT

CENTRE-SPREAD PHOTOGRAPH BETWEEN PAGES 176 AND 177

20–30 mangetout peas
2 tablespoons groundnut oil
450g (1lb) boned pork
   shoulder, very finely
   chopped or minced
2 shallots, finely chopped

2 teaspoons grated fresh root
   ginger
2–3 tablespoons dry sherry
Salt
Freshly ground black pepper
Good helping of white wine
   vinegar, for basting

Blanch the mangetout in boiling water for a maximum of half a minute. Drain and rinse under cold running water and dry well.

Heat the oil in a pan that has a lid and cook the pork and shallots for about 5 minutes until browned. Add the ginger, sherry and season to taste. Cover and cook gently for about 20 minutes, or until tender. Baste with the vinegar from time to time to stop the mixture becoming too dry. Allow to become cold. Slit the mangetout open along one side and stuff generously with the pork filling.

PORK SPRING ROLLS
Vietnam

350g (12oz) lean pork, such as
    tenderloin, cut into very
    thin strips
350g (12oz) beansprouts
4 chestnut, shiitake or oyster
    mushrooms, finely chopped
3 spring onions, finely
    chopped
1 teaspoon soft brown sugar

Salt
1 teaspoon cornflour
1 tablespoon dark soy sauce
Vegetable oil for deep-frying
2 teaspoons chopped fresh root
    ginger
2 cloves garlic, finely chopped
Rice papers for wrapping
A little beaten egg

Put the pork, beansprouts, mushrooms, spring onions, sugar and salt in a large bowl and toss well together. Blend the cornflour with the soy sauce and stir it into the pork mixture. Leave to marinate for not less than 30 minutes.

Heat 2 tablespoons oil in a wok or frying pan. Stir-fry the ginger and garlic over a high heat for a minute.

Add the pork, vegetables and marinade and stir-fry for 4 minutes, until most of the liquid has disappeared and the pork is cooked. Allow to cool.

Dip the rice papers one at a time into cold water to soften them and pat dry with a kitchen towel. Place a spoonful of pork mixture in the centre of each rice paper. Fold the edge nearest you to the centre. Fold both sides in towards the centre, then roll up, sealing the last edge with a little beaten egg. Make all the rolls in a similar way.

Heat about 5cm (2 inches) oil in a wok or deep-frying pan and deep-fry the pork rolls, a few at a time, for 2–4 minutes, or until golden brown. Turn the rolls during cooking to ensure even browning. Drain well on kitchen paper and eat warm.

BASIC SAUCES, PASTES AND STOCKS

NUOC CHAM
Vietnam

1 red chilli pepper, seeded and
   chopped
2 cloves garlic, chopped
4 teaspoons brown sugar

4 tablespoons fish sauce
5 tablespoons water (or more
   if you like)
Juice of ½ fresh lime

Pound the chilli, garlic and sugar using a pestle and mortar. (An electric blender will not give the right consistency.) Stir in the fish sauce. Add the water and the lime juice, blending well.

Nuoc cham can be stored in the refrigerator for up to a week.

TAMARIND SAUCE
Vietnam

This is particularly good with seafood.

4 tablespoons tamarind
   concentrate, dissolved in
   225ml (8fl oz) boiling water
1 teaspoon brown sugar

2 tablespoons fish sauce
2 large red chilli peppers,
   seeded and very finely
   chopped

Put the dissolved tamarind concentrate into a bowl. Add the sugar and fish sauce to the tamarind and mix it well to dissolve the sugar.

Garnish with the chillies.

RED CURRY PASTE
Thailand

10–12 red chilli peppers, seeded
6 cloves garlic
2–3 tablespoons finely chopped onion
1 tablespoon chopped lemon grass
1 tablespoon chopped fresh root ginger
1 tablespoon chopped fresh coriander
Dash of shrimp paste
Couple of good pinches of ground cumin
Salt
3 tablespoons groundnut oil

Put everything except the oil into a blender or food processor and whizz until smooth.

Heat the oil in a pan and slowly fry your curry paste for a few minutes to release the aroma. Store in a lidded jar in the fridge for up to 4 weeks.

Hotness will vary according to the type of chillies used. You can add a few seeds if you like it very hot.

GREEN CURRY PASTE
Thailand

About 15 green chilli peppers, seeded
1 head of garlic – about 8 cloves
2 blades of lemon grass, cut into small pieces
1 tablespoon sliced fresh root ginger
1 tablespoon chopped shallot
3 tablespoons fresh chopped coriander (preferably root)
Couple of good pinches of ground cumin
Dash of shrimp paste
Juice of half a lemon

Put all the ingredients into a blender or food processor and whizz until smooth. Alternatively, you can pound everything together in a pestle and mortar. The paste will keep in an airtight container in the fridge for up to 4 weeks.

The hotness will vary according to the heat of the chillies and you can add some seeds if you like it very hot.

MALAYSIAN CUCUMBER PICKLE

CENTRE-SPREAD PHOTOGRAPH BETWEEN PAGES 112 AND 113

This wonderful pickle is best left for 24 hours before being eaten – if you can resist it. It'll keep well for over a week in the fridge.

2 cucumbers, cut into 2.5cm (1 inch) sticks (peel first if you are using a thick-skinned, ridged cucumber)
1 carrot, cut into 2.5cm (1 inch) sticks
1 onion, finely chopped
1 red chilli pepper, seeded and chopped
2 tablespoons salt
3 cloves garlic, chopped
6–8 shallots, chopped
6–8 dried red chilli peppers, chopped
2.5cm (1 inch) piece of fresh root ginger, chopped

2 Brazil or 4 macadamia or cashew nuts
3 tablespoons groundnut oil
Scant teaspoon mustard seeds
2 generous pinches of ground turmeric
3 tablespoons whole dried prawns, ground – rinse them before use
3 rounded tablespoons white or brown sugar
175ml (6fl oz) white wine vinegar

Put the cucumbers, carrot, onion and chilli into a dish and sprinkle with salt. Leave to marinate for a couple of hours. Rinse well and dry with kitchen paper.

Using a pestle and mortar or blender, grind the garlic, shallots, dried chillies, ginger and nuts to a paste.

Heat the oil in a pan and fry the mustard seeds for a few seconds. Add the ground ingredients and the turmeric and cook for about 4 minutes. Pop in the dried prawns and cook for 2 minutes, then add the sugar and vinegar.

Cook gently until the mixture becomes quite thick. Adjust the seasoning if necessary. Add the marinated vegetables and toss like a salad. Remove from the heat and allow to cool before spooning into warm clean jars.

VEGETABLE STOCK

MAKES ABOUT 1.2 LITRES (2 PINTS)

1 large onion, stuck with
  whole cloves
2 carrots, sliced
2 leeks, chopped
Bouquet garni
Wedge of lemon

725ml (1¼ pints) water
725ml (1¼ pints) dry white
  wine or dry cider
1 tablespoon white wine
  vinegar

Put all the ingredients into a large pan. Bring to the boil, then reduce
the heat, cover and simmer for about 30 minutes. Cool slightly, then
strain through a very fine sieve. Cool completely, refrigerate and use
within 2 days, or freeze and keep for up to 3 months.

THAI SOUP STOCK

MAKES 1.5 LITRES (2½–3½ PINTS)

2.25 litres (4 pints) water
700g (1½lb) chicken, beef,
  pork or fish bones,
  depending on the flavour of
  the stock you need
2 sticks of celery, chopped
2 onions, chopped

2 fresh coriander roots,
  chopped
4 Kaffir lime leaves
2.5cm (1 inch) piece of fresh
  root ginger, chopped
Salt
Freshly ground black pepper

Put all the ingredients into a very large pan. Bring to the boil, then
reduce the heat and simmer, covered, for about 1 hour, skimming the
fat from the surface from time to time.

Strain through a fine sieve and discard all but the stock, then strain
again, lining the sieve with muslin to achieve a clear liquid. Cool and
refrigerate, then skim off any fat from the surface. Use within 2 days,
or freeze and keep for up to 3 months. Use in the soup recipes.

FLOYD'S TRAVEL TIPS

MALACCA

■ This is the first in what I hope will be a series of Floyd's TRAVEL TIPS. On arriving at a strange hotel tired and late at night, don't tip the man who greets you so effusively. He won't be on duty tomorrow and you'll have to do it all over again.

■ Go to bed by elevator and go to work by the stairs. This way you'll keep fit!

■ One evening we had to complain bitterly at our Malacca hotel about our steak being absolute crap, and the only response was they were very sorry but they couldn't deal with us unless we filled in a questionnaire – which asked what we thought of the decor, attitude of staff, quality of service, quality of food, presentation, value for money. I suggest that when faced with one yourself, in the bit for the staff, you must put ticks in the 'excellent' boxes for friendliness, politeness, service – then, unequivocally slag off the food, thus not denting the egos of the people who tomorrow you might want a favour from.

■ Always try to stay in a hotel that's far too expensive or too small for large tour groups to visit. There is nothing more irritating than the group leader coming round distributing photographs to the tables at lunch, etc., etc.

■ Before you attempt the hotel's grill, its Asian speciality room, its cooking corner and all the rest of it, just order egg and chips. If that happens well, keep eating there. If they can't do it, change your hotel.

HONG KONG

■ As soon as you have established a table in the dining room, cover it completely with cigarettes and lighters, so that the blind American who comes in and can't see the 'no smoking' area clearly designated on the other side of the room doesn't sit next to you and start becoming a pain in the ass.

■ When your partner leaves the lunch table to go and make an important telephone call and may be away for some time, communicate this immediately to the staff, because you might want to carry on eating your pudding and they will, of course, use this excuse for not coming near you for the whole time that your partner is absent. Thus, in fact, delaying the whole process that you are trying to speed up.

■ At every luxury hotel you stay in pinch all the little boxed toothbrushes, the hair shampoo, the special slippers with the hotel's monogram on them and stuff like that. By the end of the year, if, like me, you stay 200 nights a year in a hotel, you'll have truckful of really useful stocking fillers for Christmas presents.

■ Always carry one of those pencil-slim pocket torches.

■ Never reveal to anybody your exact schedule. You'll find they're either waiting there to harass you the next day or to demand a tip.

■ When your joined by others at the bar after you've just ordered a round, sign your cheque or settle in cash immediately – so when the next person gaily asks for a drink, it doesn't go on your bill. And after everyone has gone you won't be left to pay for seventeen drinks no one has really thought about paying for.

■ Be firm with taylors!

■ Always carry a newspaper!

VIETNAM

■ To return to the subject of collecting all the toothbrushes and hotel goodies for Christmas presents and stocking fillers – always pinch the goodies on the first night you arrive. The following morning they'll think they didn't provide any for you and replace them.

■ While travelling in the East, a little supply of toothpicks is indispensable. Therefore, have a small silver toothpick made for yourself so you don't have to rummage round in the bottom of your Samsonite bag for something you pinched off the last airline.

■ I must design a gentleman's portable ashtray. It would be the size of a 2oz tin of Golden Virginia and in the lid, which would lift off anyway, there would be a little flip-up like a Jaguar and Bentley car ashtray. And then you could carry it on boats and in places where you can't smoke and empty it out later into a litter bin. I could make a fortune.

INDEX